justified secrets

tfh team bravo
book one

Melissa Schroeder

cover art by
Scott Carpenter

edited by
Noel Varner

Harmless Publishing

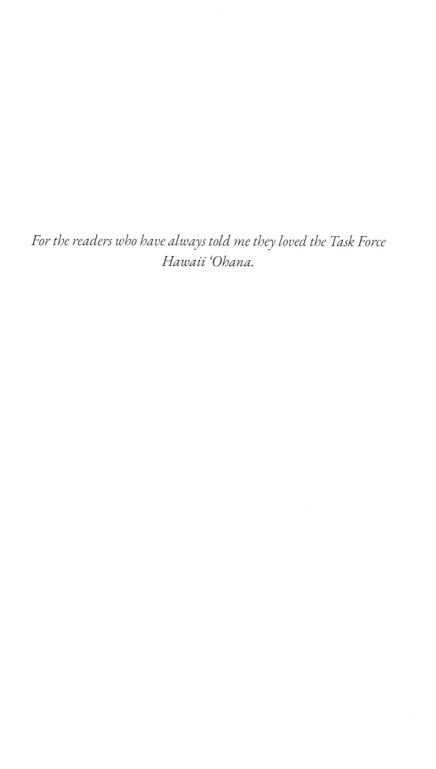

For the readers who have always told me they loved the Task Force Hawaii ʻOhana.

contents

also by melissa schroeder

- Infatuation
- Possession
- Surrender

Task Force Hawaii

- Seductive Reasoning
- Hostile Desires
- Constant Craving
- Tangled Passions
- Wicked Temptations
- Twisted Emotions

TFH Team Bravo

- Justified Secrets

THE CAMOS AND CUPCAKES WORLD

Camos and Cupcakes

- Delicious
- Luscious
- Scrumptious

The Fillmore Siblings

- Hate to Love You
- Love to Hate You

Juniper Springs

- Wild Love

- Crazy Love
- Last Love
- Imperfect Love

THE SANTINI WORLD

The Santinis

- Leonardo
- Marco
- Gianni
- Vicente
- A Santini Christmas
- A Santini in Love
- Falling for a Santini
- One Night with a Santini
- A Santini Takes the Fall
- A Santini's Heart
- Loving a Santini

Semper Fi Marines

- Tease Me
- Tempt Me
- Touch Me

The Fitzpatricks

- Chances Are

THE MELISSA SCHROEDER INSTALOVE COLLECTION

Dominion Rockstar Romance

- Undeniable
- Unpredictable
- Unexpected
- Tempted

Mafia Sisters

- Stealing Destiny
- Guarding Fable

Faking It

- Faking it with my Billionaire Boss
- Faking it with my Brother's Best Friend
- Faking it with my Frenemy

The Fighting Sullivans

- Falling for the General's Daughter
- Falling for the Girl Next Door
- Falling for my Best Friend
- Falling for my Baby Mama

Also Included

- Kiss my Tinsel
- Dad Bod Rockstar

Texas Temptations

- Conquering India

- Delilah's Downfall

Hawaiian Holidays

- Mele Kalikimaka, Baby
- Sex on the Beach
- Getting Lei'd

Once Upon an Accident

- The Accidental Countess
- Lessons in Seduction
- The Spy Who Loved Her

The Cursed Clan

- Callum
- Angus
- Logan
- Fletcher
- Anice

The Sweet Shoppe

- Tempting Prudence
- Cowboy Up
- Her Wicked Warrior

Lonestar Wolf Pack

- Primal Instincts

Texas Heat

- Scorched

Spies, Lies, and Alibis

- The Boss

SINGLE TITLES

- A Calculated Seduction
- Chasing Luck
- Going for Eight
- Grace Under Pressure
- Operation Love
- Saving Thea
- Snowbound Seduction
- Sweet Patience
- The Last Detail
- The Seduction of Widow McEwan

hawaiian terms

Aloha - Hello, goodbye, love

Bra-Bro

Bruddah- brother, term of endearment

Haole-Newcomer to the islands

Howzit - How is it going?

Kamaʻāina-Local to the islands

Mahalo-Thank you

Malasadas- A Portuguese donut without a hole which started out as a tradition for Shrove (Fat) Tuesday. They are deep fried, dipped in sugar or cinnamon and sugar. In other words, it is a decadent treat every person must try when they go to Hawaii. If you do not try it, you fail. Do yourself a favor. Go to Leonard's and buy one. You are welcome.

Pupule - crazy

Slippahs - slippers, AKA sandals

prologue

16 years ago

"SUMMER," her mother whispered, her voice harsh and full of anxiety. It wasn't anything new. Joseph was a monster. Her mother lived in a constant state of terror. Everyone at the compound did.

"It's time to go."

Summer blinked, trying to get her mind to focus. "What?"

"Let's go. We need to go."

For a long moment, her brain swam in confusion as if it were drowning in denial. Then, finally, something clicked, and she sprang into action. They had planned this for over a month, and it was finally happening.

She grabbed her go-bag and her shoes and ran to join her mother. Silently, they slipped down the hall, their bare feet barely making a noise. They moved like that until they reached the outside of the building. It was cooler outside, a light trade wind dancing over her hair. Fudge, she should have put her hair up. It was too late, but she would fix it when they were free of this cursed compound.

Crowding their bodies up against the outside wall of the house, they made their way to the back of their dwelling. They were lucky that her mother was the only woman legitimately married to Joseph, which afforded them the two-room "house." It was more of a condo with no real kitchen, but it was better than one of the many multifamily units. Those were crowded with people.

Her mother raised her hand. Summer held her breath. The seconds ticked by...the silence surrounding them as fear pounded in her head. She knew it had only been a few seconds, but it felt as if she would die if she didn't take a breath in the next few milliseconds.

Finally, her mother waved her hand. Summer gulped in air as she followed her mother. Their house backed up to the fields, giving them an easy way out if they could avoid the patrols.

Her mother stopped and slipped on her shoes, and Summer followed suit. They hurried to the taller crops that would give them cover as they stole away from Joseph.

They were almost to the edge of their property when the shouts went up, with the sirens sounding. Panic hit her first as they picked up their pace, running and not caring how much noise they made. Their pursuers were getting closer, then they heard the four-wheelers.

Her mother stopped so abruptly that Summer ran into her.

"Oof," Summer said.

Her mother took Summer by her upper arms and propelled her forward.

"Go. There will be a man named Sam Smith. He will take you somewhere safe."

"Where are the other girls, Mama?"

She shook her head, her tired eyes filling with tears. "I couldn't get them out. Just you."

"No!"

"I know you don't think much of me, but you must go. Sam's an old friend. He knows who you are. Go with him. He will explain everything. Just run straight ahead. He should be waiting on that dirt road back there."

"What does he look like?"

"He's tall, handsome, with dark hair and amber eyes. Go." Her mother pulled her into a hug so tight Summer almost stopped breathing. "Make sure you tell people. We need to save those girls."

Then, her mother turned and cut across the fields, leading the idiots on a chase. Tears filled Summer's eyes. Her mother had just sacrificed herself. Joseph wouldn't hesitate to torture her.

"She's moving North now," Amos yelled out. That guy was a moron.

Knowing that she had to move, or she would end up back on the compound, she turned and ran as fast as she could, knowing those pinheads would pursue her mother and not send scouts out to make sure they hadn't split up.

Her side was hurting by the time she arrived on the dirt road.

"Woah," a cultured English voice said as a man approached her. "Are you okay, love?"

She looked up at the man. Salt and pepper hair, big, strong...and amber eyes.

"What's your name?"

He nodded as if he approved of her question. "Sam Smith. Where's your mother?"

Her eyes filled with tears again. "The guards realized we left too soon. She's distracting them. Can we wait?"

He looked over her head at the fields behind her, the noise of the engines still blaring but further away.

"No. I would like to, love, but Nora made me promise to get you out of here and off the island."

She swallowed the need to argue. One thing everyone at Joyous Wave understood was that arguing could have dire consequences, especially with older men.

"Let's get off this island and then release the news."

"What?"

"Sorry, I thought your mother told you. If she didn't get out of there, I would release the news and let everyone know what has been going on so we can hopefully save your mother and the other girls. But she wanted you off the island."

"They'll see us at the airport."

He smiled a flash of white against the dark Hawaiian night. "Good thing I have my boat. Let's go, Summer."

"I don't want to be called Summer."

He blinked. "Okay, we can talk about that later."

She followed him to the Jeep and climbed in. Within twenty minutes, they arrived at the dock. The boat was a yacht with an entire staff onboard. "Mr. Smith, we're ready to leave as soon as you give us the word."

"Now. We go before any of those bastards can figure out where I took her."

"Yes, sir," he said, hurrying away.

"Come, are you hungry? I ensured there was food here because Nora said you would be hungry."

As if to prove her mother's point, her stomach growled. He smiled. He had a kind one, not calculated, but filled with good humor.

"Who are you?"

He sighed and motioned with his head. "Let's go and grab something to eat. It's a long story."

The moment she stepped into the galley, her eyes bugged out. It was opulent and nicer than anything she had ever seen, but then she'd spent almost every minute of her life at Joyous Wave. While Joseph lived in luxury, the majority of the cult lived in barely standing huts that leaked in rain showers and drowned them in storms.

"Have a seat...wait, what do you want to be called?"

She blinked, then remembered that she had declared she wanted to change her name. "I don't know. I always hated the name, though."

He smiled. "But you were born in the Summer."

She rolled her eyes. "Sounds like a Joseph idea."

His smile faded. "I wish your mother would have called for me. I just didn't know about you, about where she was. I knew she was married to Joseph, but I didn't know."

"You knew my mother before Joseph?"

He nodded as he handed her a glass of water. "I have soda, too."

She'd never had soda before. "My mother?"

"Right. Sorry. You look so much like Nora."

"Are we related?"

"Why do you ask?"

"We have the same eyes. Are you a distant relative to my mother?"

He shook his head. Sadness filled his gaze. "No. But I am

related to you, and I will explain everything to you, but let me fix you some food first."

She nodded and looked out the window. Maui grew smaller and smaller into the distance as Sam puttered around the galley. She prayed that her mother would be safe, that she could lie and tell Joseph that she had been chasing Summer. In her heart, though, Summer knew terrible things would happen.

She just didn't know how bad it would be and how many of her friends would die.

one

Present Day

"AUTUMN, ARE YOU WITH ME?"

Autumn blinked, her gaze focusing on Jin Phillips, soon-to-be Jin Lee. It took her a moment to bring the present back into focus. Jin smiled at her, her kind expression relaxing Autumn's nerves. Not that Jin would have picked up on it. Autumn learned at an early age to hide her emotions.

Her boss's fiancée hosted *Beyond Murder*, a cold case podcast that went beyond just the nitty gritty most true crime shows talked about. As someone who had been the subject of many true crime shows, Jin understood there was more to every story.

Her interest in Autumn came from a case Task Force Hawaii had all worked on a few months earlier. It was then that she had come to Autumn about recording a podcast about her time at Joyous Wave. Autumn had planned on avoiding the subject, but she knew there was one thing that would bring out Joseph: Autumn spilling all his secrets.

"Sorry, I was woolgathering."

"No problem. If you aren't up to talking today, we can handle this another day."

She shook her head. Autumn was usually better at ignoring the memories, but since Joseph's minions had popped back up a few months ago and wreaked havoc on the island, she'd been falling back into those wretched memories. It had not surprised her that Joseph was entangled in drug smuggling and murders.

"Let's talk about your name change."

Autumn smiled. That was an easy answer. "Rumors were Joseph picked my name."

"And you didn't want any connection to him." Not a question, because Jin researched the people she would interview. "You even went back to your mother's maiden name."

"Officially, I was never a Watters. Joseph wasn't on any of my identification." She shrugged. "Truth?"

Jin nodded. "Always."

"I didn't even have a birth certificate when I ran away from Joyous Wave."

"You mean on you. Was it destroyed in the explosion?"

"I mean, I didn't have one. None. Not that I know of. Nothing was ever filed with the state. I was born on the compound, so there was no official record of my birth."

Jin blinked. "You're kidding me."

She shook her head. "I have no idea why the other kids did. But I was the first born there, so that might be why. Anyway, once I escaped, I had the choice of what name to put on my birth certificate." It had taken her a few weeks to decide, flinching every time someone said her name.

"And you chose another season. Any particular reason?"

"It's the season Sam Smith met my mother. And since he

saved me, I thought it was a great way to honor him and my mother."

"Your connection to the Smiths, they adopted you?"

"Yes. Although my brother," she said, using air quotes, "wasn't thrilled, I totally understood. His mother had just died six months earlier, and here comes this weird girl who didn't know how to operate a computer, let alone how to function in the real world, taking up his father's time."

Another pause from Jin. This is why Autumn rarely talked about Joyous Wave. People were astonished that she had been so backward. "You didn't know anything about computers?"

The old embarrassment threatened to rise up again, but she forced it back. "*Tools of the Devil,* according to Joseph. He used them, but he was the leader, right? I think the entire circle—meaning the stupid men—all had access to them."

"Your education was stunted?"

"That's a nice way of putting it. I was lucky that my mother was teaching me things on the side. Reading for women was allowed, but only scripture."

"The Bible?"

"No, *scripture*. The nut bag had his version of the bible, which was all about him being the Messiah. Want to know a secret?"

"Again, always."

"Joseph was a conman, from start to finish. He never believed he was there to rescue people. He was there to prey upon them."

"Aren't most cult leaders that way?"

"To an extent, but I'm convinced Joseph started Joyous Wave to make money. He was a drug dealer before, during, and after Joyous Wave."

Jin studied her for a long moment. Again, it was the same look she got from almost everyone when she talked about Joseph still being alive. According to the FBI, Joseph Watters was dead.

"So, back to your brother. He's younger?"

"Yes, by about two years."

As if on cue, her phone buzzed on the table. She knew without looking who it was.

> Ian: I said not to do the interview, and you ignored me. WTH?!

She was positive he had some kind of tracker on her or her phone. How did he find things out so fast? It wouldn't be the first time he did it, but it had been years. When she had been undercover as a DEA agent, Ian had been so overprotective. Even as he traipsed the world as a spy for the British government, he somehow kept track of her. After discovering Joseph was back on the islands, he started playing the mother hen again.

"Do you need to take that?"

"No." It buzzed again, and she turned it over. He should know after all these years that he had no control over her. "What else do you want to know?"

She climbed the stairs to her apartment, dreading her showdown with Ian. The moment her foot hit the landing for her floor, two doors opened. Ian stepped out of her apartment, glowering in a way most women would find sexy. She did not.

The other door was Freddy's. His wrinkled face probably

came from his time in the sun and the drugs he had taken over the years. The truth was, she had no idea how old he was. Over the last eighteen months, though, she had formed a relationship with him. She paid him for news on the streets about new drugs or dealers.

He smiled at her, showing off his three missing teeth. From his facial features, she knew he was at least a quarter Asian, with dark hair that needed a good wash. He had a scar on his right jaw that looked like it was from a knife. He stood at least three inches shorter than her.

"Hey, pretty Autumn."

"Hey, Freddy. Howzit?"

He frowned. "Not sure."

That was a regular thing. Freddy was still using, and at this point in his life, she wasn't sure he would ever be able to beat the addiction. He had a thing for crack, and it had left his brain mushy. She never knew when she might find him dead, but she knew that day was coming.

"Did you have something for me?"

"Other than that pretty boy giving you the look of death?"

She smiled. Freddy was gay and had a thing for Ian. He talked about her best friend/brother incessantly.

"Yeah, other than that. That I deserve, but don't worry. I know how to handle him."

"I could handle him, too."

She barked out a laugh. "Stop that. You sure you haven't heard anything?"

"Not anything yet, but there's word about a new synthetic on the streets."

She ordered her heart to settle the hell down. There was always something new on the islands, and it didn't mean it was

Joseph. The former cult leader loved to deal synthetics, but so did a lot of other bastards.

"Find out where they're selling it, okay?"

He nodded and turned back into his apartment.

"Wait."

Freddy turned around to look at her.

"When was the last time you ate, Freddy?"

"Don't worry about that, pretty Autumn. I'll get you the info as soon as I can."

"No," she stepped forward and dug into her back pocket for a gift card to a local fast-food place. She had them on hand to give to kids on the streets. That way, she knew they would at least get food and not drugs. She held it out and waited. Freddy was the weirdest informant she'd ever had. The man honestly didn't ask for more than he deserved.

"You don't need to give me that."

"I know. But I'll shove it under your door, so save me the trouble and get something to eat."

He hesitated, then took it. "Deduct it from my payment."

"Can't. The money has to be allocated to you, and I would be breaking the law if I did that."

That was a lie. The money Autumn gave him came from her own pocket, but Freddy didn't need to know that.

"Thanks."

He acted like she had given him the most precious gift, and it hurt her heart. People like Freddy were preyed upon by drug dealers and manufacturers. Yes, they were weak to start using. Still, if people like Joseph weren't around manufacturing and selling drugs, they might have found help elsewhere.

She pushed those thoughts aside and turned to head for her apartment. Ian was still glowering at her. Women always lost their heads around him, probably because they didn't know what a pain in the ass he could be. It was the midnight dark hair, blue eyes...and that stupid accent. It irritated her that she couldn't mimic it well. Southern US was about as far as she could get in accents.

"What the bloody hell did you just do?"

"I gave Freddy a gift card for L and L. Are you jealous? I can give you one."

A flush started at his throat and then filled his cheeks. He was her brother, and she loved messing with him. It was fun to watch the former MI-6 agent lose it.

"I'm not talking about that. I'm talking about you being at Jin's."

She rolled her eyes. "No need to get your panties in a twist."

"We talked about this and agreed it was a bad idea."

"First," she said, stepping over the threshold of her apartment, "I didn't agree. You agreed with yourself."

"Dad agreed."

She glanced at him. "Should we call him and check?"

He hesitated.

"That's what I thought. Ian, it's been months since we knew for sure Joseph was back on the island. He hasn't made a move."

She could feel the former cult leader circling her like the shark that he was. He loved head games, so she refused to let him see that it gave her the freaks. By doing the interview, she hoped it would trigger him.

"So you think participating in a podcast that will call him out is a good idea?"

He didn't even try to hide the sarcasm in his voice.

"Do you have another idea? Sitting here waiting for that

bastard to make a move is not the smartest thing. That's playing his game."

This argument was tiring her out. Every time they got together lately, they ended up in a fight about it. She wasn't going to change her mind. This was the only way to draw out that bastard. The only thing she was thankful for was that her brother and father believed her. Most people would nod and ask questions, but there was always a hint of disbelief in their voice that Joseph was still alive.

"And what do you call this?"

"Checkmate."

He sighed. She hated discussing this with Ian. He always took it to heart that she might get hurt. She knew there was a ninety-nine percent chance she wouldn't make it out of this alive. She knew what Joseph was after. The only way he achieved his success was if she were dead. At least if he still believed he was her biological father.

"Did you really tell Dad?"

He shook his head. "He's got enough on his hands right now."

Sam was moving to Hawaii. He'd had a kidney transplant four months ago and decided that life was too short to keep working. With both her and Ian living on Oahu, he picked Honolulu as his new home. It seemed like out of the blue, but Sam was like that. He would brood about something for months before making a decision. The problem was that, in most cases, his actions would put him in harm's way—especially if Ian or she were involved.

"Why is he coming here?"

"You know. He wants to be close to us."

Yeah, she understood that, but there was something else

going on with him. Everything had been surface talk lately. He would ask about her job, about the weather…but nothing else. It made her suspicious of his true reason for coming to Hawaii. Probably because they didn't know her entire plan. And if she worried about it too much, Ian would pick up on it.

"I'm hungry."

"Color me surprised."

Again, sarcasm. Truthfully, she understood it. Her metabolism mimicked a hobbit's. Autumn was convinced that it had to do with her sixteen years in a cult. There was never enough food when she was a kid.

"Let's get something to eat," she said.

"You could cook." One little-known fact about her was her love of cooking. It was something she'd learned after leaving the cult. Since she had to be tutored from home for the first year, she'd spent a lot of time watching TV, which was when she discovered cooking shows.

"Not in that kitchen. It's a death trap."

He followed her out of the door and onto the landing. She locked her door, although she was sure anyone could break in. It's why she rented it.

"I mean at the other place."

She stopped in her tracks and glanced over her shoulder at him. "No. I need to limit my time there now that we know Dear Leader is back on the islands."

He nodded in understanding. She would not lead Joseph there.

"I think I need a big meal."

"You always need a big meal," he said, following her to his car. She was really amazed it still had the tires left. She'd picked this apartment building because it was close to work, and she didn't care if people broke in.

"Where do you want to go?"

She checked the time and realized it was almost six. No wonder she was hungry. And that meant no Liliha Bakery. Bummer.

"Hmm, not sure. Do we want local cuisine or something else?"

"I don't care, just not a dive bar. I think that last one gave me food poisoning."

"It did not. It was all the alcohol."

He cut her a glance but kept driving.

"I know. Let's hit up that taco place in Aiea. The one in the gas station. Amanda and Felix went there one time, and it looked amazing."

"I need to block that channel."

"Go like you're heading to Bravo's."

"Just for the record, I think you need help with your food fixation," he said as he took the Pali to get on the interstate.

"I don't have a food fixation." She totally did.

"Have you ever noticed that you give directions by restaurant or food truck?"

She frowned. "I do?"

Ian laughed. "Yeah. And why are we going to a gas station to eat?"

"It used to be a gas station, you'll see."

He grumbled but headed in the direction of Aiea. She needed some good food and time with her brother not talking about her childhood.

two

SETH HARRISON LOOKED around the table at his team. He had done his best to make sure to build the camaraderie. At least once a week, they met up for drinks or dinner. Or drinks AND dinner.

"I'm ready for our first weekend to cover for Alpha," Robbie Ramirez said. He had the good looks of his father—his words, not Seth's—who was Mexican, and his mother's eyes, who was Italian. The former SEAL had been on Team Six—the one no one is supposed to know about. He had the same build as when he was a SEAL and was always looking for action—at work and at play.

"Jesus, Rami, don't jinx us," Nikki Kekoa, the former Coastie who originally hailed from Maui, said. Since that was the island they usually covered, he thought it had been a stroke of luck she had applied. She'd pushed all her dark hair from her face, making her appear younger than she was. He knew that she used that to her advantages in the field.

"There are no such things as jinxes," former NCIS agent Kapone Hanson said. He drawled out the words in his southern twang that he bumped up whenever Kap was romancing women or when he'd had a few beers. It didn't hurt that he was taller than Seth, who came in at 6'3".

"You deal with your weird mainland things, and I'll be in charge of the local legends," she quipped back. "And Rami, don't give us bad juju for next weekend."

Seth glanced at the quietest of the group, Ryan Morrison. He was former LAPD, and Maya, his SAR dog, was at his side. Morrison looked like he should be playing volleyball or in a movie on the beach. He had those good looks that turned the heads of many women, with one of those square jaws, deep blue eyes, and messy blond hair.

"Woah, TFH, three o'clock," Rami said.

Seth turned around and immediately wanted to curse. Autumn Bradford was making her way from an expensive sports car with Ian Smith. The former MI-6 agent seemed to be her constant companion. When she saw them, she smiled, one of those amazing smiles that always caught his breath in his chest.

They changed directions and made their way through the patrons to their table.

"Hey, Bravo, howzit?"

Every now and then, he forgot that while she'd spent all of her childhood in a cult, she was from Hawaii originally.

"Going okay," Kapone said, his accent thick and his smile widening. Fucker.

She laughed but said nothing else.

"Are you here by yourselves?" Nikki asked. "And if you are, please rescue me from the sausage fest my life has become."

Autumn glanced at her companion, who had said nothing. While Bravo and Autumn were dressed in t-shirts and cargo pants, Ian was dressed as if he had somewhere else to be. The dress pants and button-down just didn't fit in with them—along with shoes he was sure were more than Seth would pay for a pair. Hell, they were probably a couple months' paycheck.

Ian nodded.

"We'll go order, then grab a couple of chairs."

They left the group.

"Do you think they're bumping uglies?" Nikki asked the group.

"Ugh, why are you the most crass of all of us?" Ramirez asked.

"Raised in a house of four boys and no mom." Nikki's mom had died when she was young, and her father didn't remarry until she was in high school. "Also, I have a set of balls while the rest of you are missing them. Either way, what are the odds?"

"Nope. I do not want any betting," Seth said.

"Why not? Alpha does it all the time," Nikki said.

Inwardly, he groaned. He loved Team Alpha. They were the original Task Force formed a few years ago. Bravo—and soon Charlie—was formed to help with the expanding need for their expertise. Team Alpha had a bad habit of betting on each other's love lives. Their commander, Martin Delano or Del, had told them to knock it off. Unfortunately, some of that rubbed off on his team during training.

"No," Ryan said quietly.

"No betting?" Nikki asked.

"No, they aren't together. Their body language is off for something like that."

They all looked at the pair. As Autumn and Ian turned, the team found something else to look at. Well, everyone but Seth.

It was always difficult to concentrate when Autumn was around. From the moment they'd met, she'd intrigued him. As they returned to their table, Nikki and Kap grabbed chairs. They all scooted around to make room between him and Nikki. When he caught her smile, he knew she had some kind of plan.

"Ian," she purred, "I heard you have a couple of the Daniels brothers working with Dillon Security."

He naturally sat down next to her to talk shop, leaving the chair next to him open. Autumn hesitated just a moment, not enough for most people to notice, but enough for him. He was tuned into her on some weird level that left him itchy. He still hadn't figured it out.

"You work today?" she asked, settling in the chair.

"Yeah. We had to run some drills and help find a tourist at Diamond Head. They overheated and had to be rescued."

She rolled her eyes. "When will they learn?"

Before he could answer, someone called out her name. She held up her hand, and the man brought her order to the table. The amount of food on the tray made his eyes widen. She shrugged. "I missed my afternoon snack."

"Maybe you should have had a snack and kept your trap shut," her companion said.

Her eyes narrowed as she cut a glance towards Ian. "Shut it, Mix."

"Don't call me that."

She smiled. "You know what they call Ian at Dillon Security? Mix. He loves that nickname."

"They do not, and I do not."

"Which one is it?" Nikki asked.

Ian opened his mouth, then he snapped it shut and frowned. "What do you mean?"

"Well, either it isn't your nickname, or it is. Can't be both."

Everyone around the table stared at him, the silence stretching out. Ian Smith was starting to discover what it was like to be part of the Task Force Hawaii family, or 'ohana as the Hawaiians called it. The silence was broken by the waiter who brought over Ian's food. Then, Seth realized that they ordered separately, meaning there was a good chance this wasn't a date. Why that made him happy, he didn't know, or he would rather not think about why it did.

"They do not call me Mix. One annoying office member uses that name, but thankfully, she's on the mainland right now."

"Emily isn't on island?" Autumn asked.

He shook his head. "She needed a break from her brothers, and Dillon needed help with personal security in Miami."

She turned to Seth. "You should see Emily. She looks like a kindergarten teacher but could take down any of the men around this table. I guess it helps when Mad Dog Daniels is your brother."

His eyebrows shot up. "The MMA fighter?"

She nodded as she took a bite of her taco. Her humming sound sent a shaft of heat spiraling through his blood. What was it about this woman? She constantly irritated and aroused him. He had never been this interested and repelled by a person.

"I might need to rethink my betting strategy," Nikki said, cutting into his infatuation. He frowned at her, a look that he knew scared people. Nikki smiled.

"What were you doing today?" Rami asked.

Autumn finished a bite of food and swallowed it before answering. "Nunya."

"Nunya?"

"Nunya business." Then, she took another healthy bite. She was rude, making everyone around the table laugh—except Ian, who looked worried.

"You don't take a lot of time off."

"I had a thing," she said. "Plus, Adam threatened that his mother would no longer make me the fried rice I love. He was lying, but I didn't want to take a chance."

"You have to be threatened to take time off?" Rami said. "You need someone to teach you how to relax."

There was no doubt from the tone in his voice what he meant. Rami had a different woman every weekend. He didn't brag, but Seth had seen him with various women at clubs. He rarely went home by himself.

"I have batteries for that."

Again, a beat of silence. Then laughter filled the air around the table. Autumn blinked as if she was confused by it. Not in a hurt way, just that she didn't realize it was a funny response. Interesting that she didn't pick up on Rami's innuendo.

"Gross," Ian said. Oh, yeah, they weren't a couple. Seth couldn't put his finger on it, but they weren't a romantic couple.

"Are y'all on call this weekend?" Autumn asked.

"We're always on call, for the most part, especially Morrison and Maya." He nodded to his dog handler. Then, Autumn realized Maya was with them since Ryan was sitting the furthest away.

She immediately forgot about her food—a first for him to witness—as she stood and hurried around the table. Dropping to her knees on the pavement, she cooed the dog.

"I'm so sorry I didn't see you here, sista." Maya licked her face, and Autumn laughed. She kissed the dog's head and then returned to her seat.

"Do you have a dog?" Seth asked.

She was still chewing her food, so she shook her head. Once she swallowed, she said, "I work too much. Not good for a dog to spend that much time alone."

The way her mouth turned down told him that she wished she could. Or maybe he was reading more into it than he should.

"I have a few cats."

"No, you feed a few strays. That's not the same thing," Ian said.

There was something in his tone, an undercurrent Seth couldn't decipher. He would bet dollars to malasadas that they weren't a couple, but there was a history there.

"Shut it, Mix. So, what's everyone doing if you aren't working this weekend?"

"You need to be careful with that Harrington," Ian said as he drove her back to her apartment.

She glanced over at him. "Why? He's a fellow team member, or rather, I don't know what we call Team Bravo, but you know what I mean."

He sped around a dilapidated minivan that looked like it would break down any minute, and her mind drifted to the team captain. Seth was...god, he was gorgeous. He had a way of looking at her with those grey eyes and all the ridiculous eyelashes around them. It was hard to understand why this man sent warmth throughout her entire body with just a look. Granted, he was a former SEAL, so his ability to hold his breath did intrigue her. But she had never really been infatuated with a man—not like this.

"He is not someone you can mess around with. I'm sure he would want to know all your secrets."

She frowned and drew her attention away from the scenery. "Do you think he has anything to do with Joyous Wave?"

"God, no. That guy would never bow down to someone like Joseph. What I mean is that he's not like us. He's normal."

She snorted to cover her hurt, but Autumn knew precisely what he meant. Ian had been raised to be a spy, and she had been raised by a narcissistic opportunist who wanted to sell her to the highest bidder after she turned sixteen.

"I understand."

"Do you?" he asked as he pulled into a parking spot near her building.

"Yeah, I do."

He sighed. "I didn't mean to be harsh."

She shook her head. "No. You're just your usual Taurus self."

"Stop with that astrology rubbish."

She laughed. "Stop being a Taurus. Later."

She kissed him on the cheek and turned to slip out of the car. He stopped her by putting a hand on her arm.

"What?"

"Be careful."

"I told you I wouldn't do anything with the SEAL."

"No. I mean, in general. There are more than likely a few eyes on you."

She offered him a small smile. "That's nothing new for me, Ian, and you know it."

She slipped out of the car and made her way to her apartment alone. As much as she loved Ian, he would never understand. She would always be alone. It was the way it had to be.

Joseph Watters watched his daughter as she shut the door to her apartment. He sighed, irritated that the surveillance cameras were the only way he could see what she was doing. At least he had that.

After Joyous Wave was reduced to rubble, he was helped by more than one of his followers, or True Believers as they liked to be called. Yes, they were idiots in many ways, but they had helped him get off the islands and somewhere safe. They were why he was sitting in an upscale condo in Waikiki with a view of Ala Moana Harbor. He was sure they had all scrapped together the millions so he could live in luxury. Of course, the pharmaceutical revenue helped.

"Why is she living there?"

He glanced at his now second-in-command. He missed Hank, but his former second-in-command had been preparing to turn evidence over for a lesser sentence. That could not be allowed, so Joseph had him killed.

This idiot, well, he was boring. Peter Moreno was in his twenties, stupid as a rock, and just about as interesting. But he was dedicated to Joseph.

"I have a feeling she has no idea of her inheritance."

There was no way his child should be living in that apartment.

It had taken him a little maneuvering to get the cameras up

in the first place. Hell, just finding out where she lived was hard enough.

"Seriously?"

He shrugged. "When Summer was stolen from me, she went into seclusion. The old man was dead then, and the money was in a trust. If no one approached her, the money just kept earning interest until she turned thirty-five, or that's what one lawyer told me."

To this day, he would never forgive his bitch of a wife for helping his daughter be stolen—especially by one of her exes. The fucking Brit would pay for it.

"Do we know if she and Smith are involved?" he asked.

"No, they are not. If they are, they hide it well."

He nodded as he rose from the chair and patted the shoulder of the young man.

"I think I will get some sleep. We have much to do tomorrow."

"Of course," he demurred as he bowed his head and stepped out of his way. Joseph wanted to roll his eyes, but he did not. He still had Joyous Wave members who thought he was their leader, and there was one thing he was sure he would need the young man's help with to exact his revenge.

But first, he needed rest, and, hopefully, the nightmares would be held at bay.

three

SETH'S PHONE woke him just as dawn was breaking over the horizon.

He reached for his phone, knocking it on the floor before he scooped it up. "Harrington."

"Is that any way to answer the phone?" his mother asked.

He would roll his eyes but wasn't awake enough for that particular activity. He collapsed back in bed.

"It's dawn, and I'm always on call."

"Oh, dammit, I forgot. Do you want me to call you back?"

His parents—especially his mother—were still adjusting to him living in Hawaii. The Navy had taken him all over the world, but now that he was in Hawaii permanently, they knew he would answer the phone. As a SEAL, he could rarely tell them what was happening—even though they both had the highest security clearance until their recent retirements. Thank God these early morning calls should stop soon.

"Naw, that's okay. What's up?"

"Well, the movers are coming Monday, and I'm not ready."

His parents had decided to move to Hawaii. His mother's sister lived on Maui, and with his two younger brothers still unmarried and in the military, his mother decided she wanted to be close to him. Seth wasn't sure if she'd consulted his father about it before she made the decision.

"Are you ever ready?"

"Yes. I'm always prepared."

His mother was brilliant, a former top-level Pentagon official who had helped plan and execute some of the most dangerous missions in the last quarter century. While he never told her where he was serving or what his SEAL team was doing, Seth had always thought she knew. That said, she was not the most organized regarding her own life. That was his father's job. The former one-star admiral kept their life orderly and on time.

"Of course."

"Don't get that tone with me, Seth."

He swallowed a laugh. "What tone?"

There was a beat of silence, then she laughed. "Sorry, I'm a little stressed about the move."

"You don't say?"

Most people would probably freak out when their parents moved halfway across the world to be closer to them—especially when they were in their thirties. But they were a military family that understood you hold onto those who love you whenever possible. Plus, he had spent nearly eighteen years in the Navy before taking the early out they'd offered him. He had his benefits, but not the top of the pay he would have gotten staying in three extra years. But, after that last mission, he knew he couldn't perform at his best for them.

"You have all of our information."

"Yes. Now, if I get called out, I'll make sure someone will pick you up."

"Seth, I'm an adult. Your father is an adult. We can hail a cab."

Yes, but they should get the whole lei treatment, in his opinion. Weirdly, his parents had never been to Hawaii.

"I know. Still, it would be nice to have someone pick you up. Unless there is an emergency, I'll probably be able to get you."

After affirming his parents' flight on Friday, he chatted about the lost tourist they had to find yesterday and then about the team. Unfortunately, he mentioned Autumn.

"There it is again," his mother said, her voice thoughtful.

"What?"

"There is a tone in your voice when you talk about that woman. Do I need to look into her?"

He was awake enough this time, so he did roll his eyes. "No. Believe me, the background check you have to do for TFH is pretty close to top-secret clearance. Plus, she worked for the DEA."

"Hmm."

"Mom, do *not* call anyone, especially Aunt Theresa."

Not really his aunt by blood, his mother's best friend worked for the DIA, the military version of the CIA.

"Okay, but I'll meet her soon enough."

With that ominous comment, she told him she had to go and hung up. He clicked off his phone and laid back on his bed. There was a good chance she was calling his Aunt Theresa right now and asking her to look into Autumn Bradford. He scrubbed his hand over his face. Maybe he should have worried about a former Pentagon official of a mother, who had nothing to do now but butt into his life. His parents had always been hands-off once their kids had hit adulthood. This would be a new experience.

His phone buzzed with a message.

Rami: *Going for a run in Waikiki. Wanna come?*

They were the two SEALs in the group and had that connection. They were never on the same team, and he was a few years ahead of Rami in SEAL training.

Seth: *Sure. Where do you want to meet up?*

Seth lived in Salt Lake, near Joint Base Pearl Harbor-Hickam. The small rental came fully furnished. He'd been stationed on Oahu but had barely spent time there. So, when he accepted the job with TFH, he decided to take his time and get to know the neighborhoods.

Rami: *On the beach by Hale Koa?*

Hale Koa was a resort for the military next to the Hilton Hawaiian Village.

Seth: *Roger that. Be there in 30.*

It was still early on a Saturday, so it wouldn't take him long to get there. He found Rami hanging out under one of the massive Banyan trees that dotted the picnic grounds between the beach and the Hale Koa.

"I take it you still work on military time too?" Rami asked.

"No. My mother still hasn't learned the time difference. You?"

He shrugged. "I had some trouble sleeping last night."

Because he was Rami's commanding officer on Team Bravo, Seth knew why he had left the military. PTSD was a bitch, but thanks to therapy, Rami was dealing with it.

"Nightmares?"

He cracked a smile. "Heartburn. But, if my mama visits, don't tell her I can't handle spicy food like I used to."

He chuckled. "Noted. And please, when my mother shows up next week, pretend you know nothing about me."

"Your folks are coming for a visit?"

He motioned toward the pathway for the run, and Rami nodded. Seth waited to answer until they were running. "No. My folks are moving here."

"Oh...damn. That sounds like a nightmare."

They split apart to get around a slowpoke couple, then came back together. "Naw, my parents have always been cool. Once we hit eighteen, they felt we were in charge of our lives. They're both retired now and with my brothers still on active duty, they decided to move near me."

"Brother, I hate to tell you, things are about to change."

Seth shook his head as they kept even pace. They ran side by side through the streets of Honolulu, the air still sweet from the night and not yet overly muggy. Even here, there was a nice trade as they took a route down Kalia Road to Ala Moana and then by the pristine shops that lined Kalakaua Boulevard. It was still quiet out, with only coffee shops and restaurants open and very few people. It had rained the night before, so the streets were mostly dry, with the occasional puddle to splash through. After passing by Duke's statue, they headed toward the zoo, then hit Kapiolani Park before hitting Diamond Head Road to loop back to the Hale Koa. By the time they arrived back on the beach, they had run for an hour.

They mainly talked about family—his brothers and Rami's little sisters—when Rami stopped mid-sentence and whistled. Rami was staring at something over Seth's shoulder, and while

Seth knew it was a woman, he wasn't prepared to see Autumn Bradford rise out of the water like some kind of Bond girl.

Damn. Of course, the woman would wear a bikini.

"Fuck," Rami said. "I mean, I knew she was gorgeous, but she hides a lot under her clothes."

That much was true. Autumn tended to wear cargo pants and t-shirts, even when they were out. Water sluiced down her stomach. Her gaze was unfocused as if she were deep in thought as she dried off. Seth thought they should leave her alone, but Rami whistled before he could say anything.

She blinked, her eyes narrowing until she realized who it was. Her expression cleared, and she smiled. Bending down, she picked up her sandals and bag and walked over to them.

"Hey, you guys out for a run this morning?"

"Yeah, and you're out for a swim," Rami said, his tone flirty.

She rolled her eyes. "I swim most mornings before the tourists show up."

"You come here every morning?"

She shrugged, which wasn't an answer. Seth felt she didn't do it at the same beach twice in a row. She walked over to one of the fountains to clean her feet off.

"You're not working, but you both drag your ass into Honolulu to exercise?"

"I live in Honolulu," Rami said.

"I live in Salt Lake. Not that far away."

She shook her head. "SEALs."

"You're one to talk. You're here swimming."

She snorted. "I do that for fun. It's a good stress release."

Rami opened his mouth with a comment that would definitely get him written up for sexual harassment, so Seth jumped in.

"All exercise is good for stress, especially with fewer tourists."

She snorted. "True. Well, I need to eat, so—"

"We could do with a bite to eat, too," Rami said, interrupting her brush-off.

"I was going to ask you."

That had Seth blinking. "You were?"

She nodded. "Although, not sure where to go. We might beat the crowds if we hit up Liliha Bakery. They have a great breakfast menu."

"Where are you parked?"

"Didn't drive. Took the bus."

Seth blinked.

"What? Are you such a snob you don't believe in public transportation?"

"Seeing that I spent most of my life in DC, I can't really be against it."

She nodded.

"I can drive you."

She eyed him suspiciously.

"Hey, if you want to ride the bus and meet us there later, go right ahead. I know Rami walked here, right?"

She glanced at the former SEAL. "Yep. I'm still in temporary quarters while I wait for the house I rented and my furniture."

"Fine, but we do it with the windows down." She dropped her bag and pulled out a pair of board shorts. After stepping into them, she tugged on a UH Warriors shirt and shoved her towel in the bag.

"Let's go. I'm hungry."

"That's nothing new," Seth said.

She laughed. "True."

They placed their orders at the counter and sat by the window in one of the booths. Autumn sat down opposite Rami. A second later, someone tapped her on her shoulder. When she looked up, she realized her mistake. Seth stood beside the booth on her side, waiting patiently for her to scoot over. She'd chosen this side, thinking keeping her distance from Rami was better. He was flirty, and she didn't mind that at all. She just didn't want to give him any ideas.

Now, she was going to be forced to sit next to the man she'd had a dirty dream about the night before.

Autumn hesitated for only a second, but it was long enough for his mouth to lift. Oh, the butthead. He knew she got antsy around him, and he was pushing it. Knowing that and wanting to prove him wrong, she scooted over.

"How long have you been living in Hawaii?" Rami asked.

"This time or before when I lived in the cult?"

For a second, he said nothing, his eyes widening. People always danced around the topic of her past. She didn't advertise it, but she didn't hide it either.

"Uhh."

She snorted. "I moved back to the islands about three years ago. I always planned on doing it, and when the job with TFH came open, I knew it was the perfect job for me where I wanted to live. Ian and Sam weren't happy, but they've learned not to get into my business."

"Ian and Sam?" Seth asked. She fought a shiver. He had one of those deep baritone voices and this slow way of talking.

He drew each syllable out, giving each sound special attention.

"Sam is Ian's father. He adopted me after I left Joyous Wave."

She could almost see the wheels turning in his head.

"So, Ian's like your brother," Rami commented.

"He *is* my brother."

"And you're why he moved here?" Seth asked.

She shrugged. "Combination of me living here and Dillon Security offering him a boatload of money." She stopped talking when the waitress showed up with their food, topping off their coffees. "Also, he's kind of a nosey Nellie."

Rami laughed. "I would love to see him when you call him that."

"How do you know I call him that to his face?"

"I have sisters. That tone," he pointed at her with his fork. "You definitely called him that to his face."

She laughed, then dug into her food, enjoying the moco loco she ordered. Her favorite recipe was her own, but if she ate out, she loved Liliha's. They had an old-school griddle where they cooked the burgers. So good.

"You seemed to be fighting last night," Seth commented as he ate his egg-white omelet. Really. At a diner. Someone needed to teach the man how to live.

"Yeah, well, we argue a lot. He's just pissed he can't control me, so it's nothing new. He wasn't happy I did an interview with Jin Phillips."

"Oh," Rami said. "About TFH?"

"No. About my time in the cult."

"Why wouldn't he want you to talk about that?" Seth asked.

She shrugged, knowing exactly why Ian didn't want her to put a target on herself. "He's worried I'll bring out the crazies. There are still *True Believers*. And, since the pandemic, true crime docs are all the rage, especially cult ones. He's worried they'll come knocking on my door."

Seth nodded as if understanding.

"So, you two go running on your days off. Lame."

Seth chuckled, the rich sound sliding down her spine. "You went swimming."

"Swimming is fun. You can pretend you're a mermaid."

Seth blinked. "You pretend to be a mermaid?"

"Sometimes." Granted, those times were usually with Del's oldest daughter, but it was fun even if she was by herself.

"Seth's life is about to get much more hectic—at least his personal life."

She glanced at Rami, then back to Seth. Damn, she didn't want to date him, but now that it sounded like he was off the market, the food in her stomach turned over. "You getting serious, SEAL?"

"Naw, my parents just retired and are moving here."

"Oh. My dad, too. He's just retired, and since Ian and I are here, and England is dreary compared to being in Hawaii, he decided to come here."

"Sam's not married?"

She shook her head. "Widowed. I never met her."

"How did he end up adopting you?"

"He and my mother knew each other in college. Sam came to the States for college."

And if her mother had never broken up with Sam, sent him away, and never met Joseph, Autumn's life would have been so different. Would she have ever met the SEAL?

"Ah, and you had no family?" He shook his head. "Sorry. I'm being intrusive."

She laughed in his face. "Don't worry, SEAL. I don't mind answering questions from fellow team members."

"Not the same team."

"No, but we're all on the same task force. I'll dig into your past and hope to get all the dirty deets from your mother."

He rolled his eyes. "There's a good chance she'll spill them."

"Good. Now, for me, no. I had no other family members. My mother was an only child to two people who were also only children. I had a few distant great aunts or something, but they were in their nineties." All she had been left with was a trust fund.

"So, Sam stepped up," Rami said.

"More than that. Sam's the one my mother called to get me out of there."

"Hmm, interesting."

"I guess." She shrugged. "He took me to England. Helped that he had connections."

"Connections?" Rami asked. She turned and looked at the former SEAL. Why couldn't she be interested in him? He would be so easy to mess with. No strings, easygoing.

"Ian is the fourth-generation spy. They have a whole family thing going on."

"Oh, that makes sense then. He could get you fake papers if need be."

"And a birth certificate if need be."

"What?" Seth asked.

"Nothing. None of it mattered because Sam had set off some fireworks by spiriting me away, which forced the FBI's hand. It caused them to move up the timing of their raid. After that FUBAR, they helped Sam get me situated."

"And you lived in England?"

"Yeah. For a few years. Went to Uni. Then moved back to the States."

"I heard you worked for the DEA," Rami mentioned.

She nodded. "Went undercover for them, but then my team was compromised. After almost being killed by a team member, I was happy to move here and work for Del and Adam."

"You were almost killed?" Seth's voice was harsh, and her eyebrows shot up.

"More than once. Goes with the undercover thing a lot, but that last time...that was bad. Ian and Sam were both jerks about it."

Granted, she'd spent over a week in the hospital after her former boss had beaten her almost to death, but she'd survived. It's what she did.

"Yeah, brothers tend to worry about their siblings being hurt." Rami laughed. "I beat up some little pissant on our street who called my sister a beaner years ago."

"Damn, I would too. Hell, I would do it today. I hate racists," she said. It was one of the things that people didn't know about Joseph. He was a raving racist. He was just a horrible human in general.

Rami smiled at her. "You and I have so much in common."

There was a low rumble beside her, and she glanced at Seth. He was frowning at his omelet—which everyone should do to egg whites, in her opinion—but she was sure the sound came from him. Then, she glanced at Rami.

"So, you were raised in a cult that was a front for a drug dealing enterprise that also sold illegal weapons?

For a long second, there was silence around the table. Then, Rami burst out laughing. When she glanced at Seth, his mouth twitched.

"You are one of a kind, Autumn Bradford," Rami said.

Taking in a deep breath, she smiled. "And my brother thanks the heavens above for that every day."

"You need a lift to your apartment?" Seth asked, hoping she said yes. It was insane how much he wanted to know where she lived. He was acting like a freaking stalker, and he had no idea why he didn't just ask her.

Nope, that was a lie. He knew. She would never tell him. When she could, he had a feeling that Autumn told the blunt truth. But she hid a lot of her motives and her life in general.

"Naw, I got someone picking me up."

Just then, the fancy sports car he'd seen at the restaurant the night before pulled into the parking lot.

"We have to get the house ready for our dad."

"I could have dropped you off."

She shook her head. "Naw. The house is on the windward side. Plus, I like making Ian bitch about sand in his hoity-toity car. See ya Monday, Bravo."

She sauntered off, and sure enough, the moment she slipped into the car, they started arguing.

"That woman has a lot of baggage."

He didn't look at Rami when he answered. "Don't we all."

They headed to his car and were on the road before Rami said anything. "It makes you think, right?"

"About what?"

"I always thought I had a shit childhood. My dad dying, all that. We were poor. But I appreciate having that over what she went through. And I'm pretty sure we don't know all of it."

"Yeah, I think she hides a lot."

"From everyone," Rami murmured.

And someone with that many secrets was a lot of work. She definitely held herself back from people while giving up all the help she could. He had witnessed it over the last few months. That meant complications, and one thing he didn't need was complications, especially with a co-worker.

four

MONDAY MORNINGS MEANT TEAM MEETINGS, and Autumn hated them. Well, hate was too strong of a word. More like she was annoyed by sitting in a room going over things. One of her many therapists—there had been a few—said that she had ADHD, which was probably true. Joseph had often attacked her lack of focus. Butthead.

"Did you just call the boss a butthead?" Charity whispered to her. The mainland transplant was as brilliant as she was beautiful. The African American scientist was their forensic tech, who dressed in the most amazing outfits. Today, she had gone all Rosie the Riveter with her hair in a bun at the nape of her neck, a red scarf with white polka dots around her head, and she was wearing an actual jumpsuit. She looked like she just walked off a movie set.

"No. I was thinking of Joseph."

Adam tossed them a look, and Autumn smiled. Adam Lee had just assumed command of Team Alpha. Del was in charge of both active teams, with a third team being formed over the next six months. Adam was the heart of TFH. A local boy who came from a long line of cops. His mother also made the best Hawaiian fried rice.

Adam started going over the plan for the week and the cases they would take on, and she fell back into her thoughts again. She wasn't on any of these particular investigations. Still, they kept abreast of what was happening with their other team members. That way, if they needed backup, they had a rudimentary idea of the investigation.

Autumn and Adam had just finished up an investigation into a new drug operation out in Wahiawa, which resulted in a significant bust.

"Also, Del, Seth, and I agreed that we needed to occasionally train on each other's teams. Since Bravo trained with us before they went into the field, we will start having individuals train with Bravo this week."

"What do you mean work with them?" Autumn asked. "I thought we already did that."

She did not need to spend any more time around Seth Harrington. It was bad enough that she'd had breakfast with him. Yes, Rami was there, but she hadn't had dreams about him all weekend. Nope. That had been Seth, and she didn't get it. Rami was the kind of guy she usually went for. No strings attached. Those kinds of men did not ask questions. Seth didn't just have strings. He would want the whole deal. Plus, she was pretty sure she wasn't his type, either.

"Del and I think knowing how Search and Rescue worked would be beneficial. Granted, none of us will take over, but it would be good to have some cross-training. And thankfully, you're free."

"Wait, what?"

"We finished up that bust last week. You have nothing else

going on, and it would be best that only one team member does the training at the time."

"You said it wasn't training."

"I said that we would not take over for them, but it would be good to understand their mission."

She wanted to roll her eyes but knew how far to push Adam. He was pretty even-tempered, but he did have his limits. Autumn learned at Joyous Wave not to poke the bear any further than needed to get your point across.

As if on cue, Team Bravo walked into the standard room. She narrowed her eyes on Seth, who smiled. Butthead. He knew she was the first one up for the training.

"If there's nothing else, let's get on with our day. Autumn, before you go off with Bravo, we need to review some of last week's particulars."

She nodded and rose from her seat to follow him into his office. She shut the door and sat down.

"Stop pouting."

"I am not pouting. Do I look like I'm pouting?"

"I know your expressions, and that one is definitely your pouting one."

Before she could respond to that nonsense—she never pouted—Del opened the door without knocking. Rude, but then he was the boss of everything.

Former special forces in the Army, Del took over TFH as soon as it was formed. He was a hunk of man, and his grumpy demeanor was only softened by his good looks. The man was a walking dream, with thick dark hair, golden brown eyes, and muscles for days.

He took the seat next to hers.

"I explained to Autumn why she would work with Bravo this week."

Del studied Adam for a long moment, and then his serious gaze cut to Autumn. Dammit. The man could take a girl down with just a look—and not in a good way.

"I believe the word you should use is ordered."

She blinked. "What?"

"You don't need an explanation. It's an order."

Ugh. She hated that, and Del knew it. She knew it was an order. Adam pretty much announced it to the group, but Del was a hard ass and didn't like any back and forth.

"I just don't want to do it."

There was a long beat of silence, then he cracked a smile. Adam laughed out loud.

"The one thing I love about you is that you are always brutally honest. Just be nice to our new team. They're all amazing law enforcement officers, and we're lucky to have them."

"Just so you know, I had dinner with them Friday night. So there."

Yep, that was mature. Seriously. Why was she freaking out? There was no reason for it. She usually enjoyed learning new things. It came from not going to a real school until she went to college. Also, Joseph thought women should only learn reading so they could read recipes. Jerk.

"Oh, really?"

"Well, Ian and I ran into them at Seafood Cartel, and we ate with them and Maya."

"I love that place," Del said. "Emma can eat her weight in tacos."

Del's wife was tiny, so there was a good chance it wasn't that much food. She remembered their last girls' night and how much Emma ate that night. Autumn realized that the woman ate almost as much as she did sometimes.

"Right? I just always want to fall face down in their Taco Cabo."

"That being said, be nice," Adam said. His voice was firm this time, and she could tell it was an order.

"Are you afraid I will hurt their feelings? I'm nice."

"You are, to a point. But like I said, you can be blunt," Adam said.

"What's wrong with being blunt? It works for Del."

Adam rolled his eyes.

"I'm the boss. I can be blunt AF if I want to."

She didn't smile, but it was hard. When she'd first met Del, he wouldn't have hesitated to use the f-word, but now that he had little ones, Autumn had noticed he had been policing his language. It was adorable.

She glanced back at Adam. "Did you make up needing to talk to me about our case?"

"No. We're going to probably go to trial. Whoever is supplying that operation has them freaked out."

"Still not understanding why they would do that," Del murmured.

"So much so that they'll go to prison instead of talk?" she asked.

"For right now. But I wanted to go over a few notes. It should only take a few minutes. Then you can go play nice with Bravo."

"Gonna stare a hole in her head, boss," Ryan said.

Seth blinked and looked at his dog handler. "What?"

He smiled, which was a rare thing for Ryan. The former LAPD was the strong, silent type. Seth understood because he knew Ryan's background. So, when he smiled, it usually made everyone around him smile.

"You're going to burn a hole in the back of her head."

"Who are you talking about?" Seth asked.

Ryan let one eyebrow rise up.

"Why would you say that?"

"Since we walked in and noticed her in Lee's office, you've barely taken your eyes off her."

He could argue with him, but Seth knew he was right. His obsession with the woman was getting worse. There was something about Autumn Bradford that drew him. He didn't understand why because she wasn't really his type. He liked the type A kind of woman because they fit his lifestyle of no attachment. She had that to a point, but there was something under the surface that he couldn't figure out. She hid so much of her past that he wanted to peel away those layers and find the soft, gooey center.

And what the hell was that thought about?

"Just gonna be interesting. You've been watching her for months."

He frowned at Ryan. "Now, what the hell does that mean?"

His cheeks felt hot, and he was worried he was blushing. Him. A man in his late thirties who had fought and killed for his country. Like a damned schoolboy.

Before Ryan could say anything else, the door to Adam's office opened, and she was striding over to them.

She wasn't overly tall, but she had long legs. When she

walked through a room, the energy shifted. At least, it did for him. From Ryan's expression, he didn't get the same vibe as Seth did.

What was *that* about?

"I've been told to play with you today."

Ryan snorted, and she smiled. Seth frowned at Ryan, who grinned at him. That was rare enough these days that it held him momentarily stunned.

"Yeah, we're not doing much today other than strength workouts."

Part of being in search and rescue was needing to be able to actually rescue people, meaning they had to carry them part, if not all, of the way.

"Cool. I need to work on my upper body anyway. Are we doing it here in the gym?"

He nodded.

"I need to change. When are we starting?"

He frowned.

"What's that for?"

"What do you mean?"

"You. You're frowning."

He smoothed out his expression. "I wasn't frowning."

"You were."

Before he could respond, Ryan decided to chime in. "You were, boss."

Deciding to ignore all that—and he was the boss, so he could—he said, "We're meeting down there in five minutes."

"See ya," she said, racing off. He blinked at how fast she was.

"She's timing herself. The girl lives for pushing herself," Marcus said. The African American was the foremost authority on the teams for terrorism. He would soon transfer to command Team Charlie.

He glanced over at the man. Marcus was an okay guy, but he did date Seth's ex, Tamilya, who was also on Team Alpha. He had no animosity towards the guy since Seth and Tamilya had broken it off years ago and had remained friends.

"That seems to be different than what she shows the world."

"No. She's irritated that someone is imposing on her time. It likely has something to do with food because that's very important to her. If she wants to have a snack break, she now has to work around Bravo's schedule. But she wants to prove to Del and Adam that she's all in for her job." He shrugged. "Probably has a lot to do with how she was raised."

Everyone knew she was the daughter of a cult leader, a man who disdained the law and definitely had a nut or two loose in that head of his.

"How so?" Ryan asked.

"Well, from the time she could probably remember, she pleased an authority figure. Del and Adam are that to her at this stage in the game. I will say she always pitches in if she can."

He had noticed that, too. She kept herself separate but on equal footing. And whenever they needed extra hands, she was there, adding to the group's overall strength. It was odd that she did so much, but many of the group knew little about her personal life. Yes, they knew she was a child of a cult leader, but beyond that—and the speculation about her relationship with Ian—people knew very little about her.

"She'll beat you down there if you aren't careful," Marcus said.

When Seth glanced over at the elevators, he noticed Ryan and Maya were already waiting on it.

"Thanks. Hey, how is the hiring for Team Charlie?"

"Got a few perspectives. It's hard since they all need the highest security clearances."

They all needed security clearances, but the terrorism group would have to have the highest because of what they would handle.

"I might have a few guys I can recommend. I know some of my old teammates are getting ready to retire."

"Hey, thanks. That would help a bunch."

"No problem."

"Are you coming, Boss?"

He glanced at the elevators again and noticed Ryan and Maya standing on the lift.

"Coming," he said, nodding to Marcus before jogging over to the lift.

"Do you think it was best to put her on that team?" Adam asked.

"She isn't on the team. She's shadowing them, and it would help if we all understood their mission. Autumn doesn't need to know exactly what they do, but understanding their mission is important."

Adam watched as she zipped out of her office and hurried to the elevators. She had some kind of bar in her hand—either candy or granola.

"But starting with Autumn?"

Del chuckled. "Yeah, risky, but it works this week. They need to feel as if they are part of the team."

"You think they don't feel like part of the team?"

"I think they do to a point. They showed up when we needed them dealing with the Hank Seymour problem."

Seymour had reportedly tried to abduct Adam's fiancée Jin a few months ago. When they zeroed in on the group they thought had her, Bravo showed up ready to help without being asked.

Del nodded. "I just want to be sure Alpha appreciates what they do. It's different from terrorism. Most will understand that, but search and rescue is slightly different."

He nodded. Each Bravo member was certified as an EMT. While the entire TFH force couldn't do that, they should understand basic rescue procedures to help in an emergency.

"Okay. But if this goes badly, I'm blaming you."

"Son, I live in a house dominated by women. I'm used to getting blamed."

Adam smiled, and then he started laughing because it was true.

"Now," Adam said, still chuckling, "why are you in my office?" He knew Del wouldn't have shown up just to talk to Autumn.

"We have an issue with a visiting dignitary who needs extra security and gave the state department and the state of Hawaii little to no warning."

That's when he saw Marcus waiting on them. He waved him in.

"So, I take it Alpha is in the hot seat for this one?"

"Yeah," Del said. "Let's get to planning."

five

AUTUMN DIDN'T WANT to go to work. It was the first time she thought about calling in sick in about a decade. The last time was when she had a dislocated shoulder. Now, she was trying to avoid a man who had haunted her dreams last night. Well, what dreams she had because she kept waking up hot and bothered throughout the night.

Still, she forced herself out of bed and into the shower to wake herself up. She needed to go shopping for food, so after throwing on some clothes and what little makeup she wore, she headed out the door to make a pit stop at Leonard's Bakery. She'd called in her order, thankful it was hot and ready when she arrived. Eating a malasada while driving to work probably wasn't a good idea, but she was starving. Lord knew what was on the agenda today.

Yesterday had been simple. Lots of exercises to build up the upper body and some practicing with dummies. Her favorite part was working with Maya. That dog was a sweetheart.

Today, Seth said something about mat exercises. That could mean so many things, but none of them were good. Once she reached TFH headquarters, she sat in her car to finish her malasada. She knew most people went for the filled malasadas these days, but she was old school. Her preference was the sugar or cinnamon and sugar. As she shoved the last bite of sugary goodness into her mouth, someone knocked on her car window.She jumped, then looked up to see her nemesis, Seth, standing there.

She went to open the door and almost hit him with it. It was his own fault since he was standing right there.

"I see your eating habits aren't any better these days."

She licked her fingers, savoring the cinnamon and sugar. When she looked up at him, he had a strange expression. "I work hard, as you know. The truth is, while I eat a lot of meals, I rarely have huge meals. Plus, I haven't had a chance to shop and needed something to eat."

She locked her door, then headed into headquarters. He fell into step with her. Of course, he did. They were going to the same place. Still, it irritated her.

"I take it you're feeling okay today."

God, his voice. How had she not noticed the way his voice slipped over each syllable?

"Yeah, I'm fine. My right shoulder feels tight, but that's probably because of an old injury."

The parking for the building was on the roof, so they stood in front of the bank of elevators, waiting for a lift.

"You should have told me," he admonished. Oh, that voice...all grumpy and ready to punish her. Would there be spankings involved?

Nope, that's inappropriate, Bradford. Stop it.

"It's nothing. And it's my own fault. I should always do PT on it, but I put that off because it kicks my ass."

"What was the injury?"

"Happened my first year at the DEA. Undercover op went bad, I ended up with damaged tendons and a dislocated shoulder."

"Damn."

"Yeah, it should have been a sign that I wasn't made for the DEA, but I don't like giving up."

"Maybe you should sit out today."

Before she could respond, the elevator dinged. He waved her on before him, such pretty manners, and she stepped on the lift. He pushed the button for the main floor. He was in what she called their work clothes, mainly cargo pants and t-shirts or polos. She was dressed similarly. Although, she was pretty sure her ass didn't look half as good as his. Every day she had to push out the image of taking a huge bite out of his ass.

Just thinking about it, about how attractive he was, and he acted like he didn't even know, pissed her off. She needed some space.

"And to answer your comment, fuck off."

"Excuse me?"

She smiled. When he got all persnickety—and yes, people should use that term more often—it made her want to ruffle his hair. He was so by the rules that she always wanted to knock him off kilter.

"Would you ask one of your team to sit it out because they might be a little sore?"

"Yes. I learned while I was an active SEAL that if you can rest and heal, you do it."

She glanced at him and saw the stark truth on his face. "No worries there, SEAL. It's a little tender, but I should be fine."

He frowned, apparently unhappy with the situation, but he

couldn't order her not to train. He would have to go to Adam or Del for that. She hoped he didn't because they would get on her ass for not doing the PT.

"It's not that important because we're going out today."

She blinked. "We are?"

"Yeah. I want to show you how we go about finding someone."

"Does that mean I get to play with Maya?"

"Work with Maya. *Work*. You don't play."

She sighed. "Fuddy duddy."

Before he could say anything, there was a buzzing. He pulled out his phone and read a text. His answer was made with angry thumbs.

"Girl from last night?"

He blinked and looked up at her. He had the most incredibly long eyelashes. It was pretty disgusting and sexy at the same time.

"No. It's my mom. They're hitting the island this week, and she's been texting me around the clock. I love her, but change is hard for her, so she has sent me many questions."

"If you don't mind me asking, what was this one?"

"If she should wear sandals on the flight. Like how would I know? And it's not like she hasn't traveled before now."

She smiled. Beneath his exasperated tone was a wealth of love. Autumn found that more attractive than his ass. Okay, not more appealing than that, but close.

"Tell her no. Wear easy slip-on and off shoes, but no sandals. You have to walk through the metal detectors in bare feet otherwise. Gross."

The elevator came to a stop, and the doors opened up. He just kept staring at her. "What?"

He shook his head. "Nothing. And thanks."

"No problem."

He followed her off the lift, typing to his mother. The rest of the group wasn't there yet or hadn't reached the main floor. Since the new teams were being drawn up, they would have their own floors. Team Bravo was one floor above them on the left side, and Charlie would take up the right side. From what she understood, their offices were done, but they were still waiting on a few things to be installed in the main conference area for Bravo.

"My mom said thanks. She had to travel for work, and we were a military family. It's like she retired and lost all sense. Again, thanks."

She smiled at him. "Anytime. I did so much traveling after I moved back to the US."

He frowned. "You didn't always live in the US?"

She shook her head. "Remember, I said Ian's dad was a friend of my mother's and I moved to England?"

"Oh, yeah. That must have been a big change."

"You have no idea, but in a way, England made it simpler. Don't get me wrong. People in the UK knew about the cult, but there wasn't as much press. Plus, Ian's dad is loaded. So, he could have round-the-clock security while I caught up."

"Caught up?"

"With school. I'd never really been to a school, so I had to do a lot of catching up. It allowed me to have a semi-normal life with no paps following me around. That probably would have happened in the US."

"Hey," Nikki said as she walked into the common area, followed by Rami. "Are we going to be doing some grappling today?"

Ugh, that would be the worst, but she would do it. She could not miss out on something like that because she had a little injury.

"No. I want to go out with Maya and show Autumn how we look for people."

Nikki frowned, but he shook his head. "I know you like doing the grappling, but we're expecting a winter storm tomorrow. Best to do those things tomorrow and stick close to base so we can go out if needed."

Winter storms on Oahu weren't what mainlanders would think of as a storm. Instead, they were harsh northern winds with rain. Sometimes, the waves got so huge they came up and over Kam Highway on the windward side.

"Hey," Nikki said, "are you going to Jin and Adam's engagement party?"

She nodded. "No way I'm missing it, although Mrs. Lee told me I can't wear cargo pants." She rolled her eyes. Adam's mom had taken her under her wing. If she could pick a mom for herself, it would be Merri Lee.

"Cool. Is this a date kind of thing?" Nikki asked.

"Why would you bring a date?" Rami asked, irritation threading his voice.

That told Autumn she was right about Rami's attraction for the former Coastie. She knew that Rami had gone through quite a few women since he'd moved to the island. She had never seen him with the same woman twice. At first, she assumed it was his nature. In her opinion, there was nothing wrong with that, but something else seemed to be going on. Like, maybe he was trying to ignore his feelings for a team member.

"Ugh, a date? First, I have to wear a dress, and now this?"

Mrs. Lee hadn't said anything about a date. She pulled out her phone and texted Adam's mother. She would tell Autumn if she needed to bring a date or not.

"Do you have a dress?" Rami asked.

"Get bent, Rami. Of course, I have a dress." She just hated to wear them. "So, do I have to bring a date? Can I just count Ian and Sam?"

"You can bring Ian any time you want to," Nikki said.

Autumn made a face. "Ugh, not you, too."

Nikki chuckled. "Well, if we're going out, I'm gonna grab my gear."

Rami stomped off after her as she headed back to the Bravo area. Their bickering faded as they rounded the corner. There were no rules about fraternization for TFH. It was allowed as long as someone wasn't in the direct chain of command, but it had to be cleared with your team leader and Del.

"So, how do you feel about team members dating?" Autumn asked, her gaze still on where the two Bravo Team members had been.

When he didn't answer, she glanced at him. He had the strangest expression on his face. "What?"

He blinked. "What?"

"I asked what you thought about team members dating."

"Oh." He said nothing for a second or two, then a flush hit his cheeks. Was he blushing? She tried not to smile, but it was hard not to. He went from being a hot former SEAL to adorable in the blink of an eye.

"Yeah, oh. I thought maybe you would have some kind of opinion since two of your team seem infatuated with each other."

He glanced over to where Rami and Nikki had disappeared, then back at Autumn. "No."

"No, you don't agree with it?"

He shook his head. "No. I mean…" He took a deep breath and seemed to center himself. "I mean that those two are not interested in relationships. Either of them."

"Oh, my sweet Summer child," she said as she patted him on the shoulder.

"What?"

"You think because both of them have said they aren't interested in relationships, they don't want them. It's cute."

"You think they're lying?"

"No. Maybe they don't want that. Maybe they're lying to themselves." She shrugged. "You never know what will happen when you meet *the* one."

Another strange look crossed over his face. "You know?"

"About meeting the one?" He nodded. "Sadly, no. But I think women in my family are destined to be alone or to be miserable because they make shitty choices."

With that, and because she felt tired and weirdly disappointed, she turned to head off to her office.

"Where are you going?"

"Need to shut down the computer and lock up my office if we're going out today."

Although he said nothing else, she was sure he didn't believe her. She didn't blame him. Even she didn't believe herself. Mainly because, for the first time in years, she wished she had another fate waiting for her. One that involved a great husband and kids.

But she knew better. Joseph wouldn't let her have that, ever.

Before she could get depressed about that, her phone buzzed. She smiled when she saw Sam's text. This Sam was not her father, Sam was the former CIA agent who drove her brother insane. She had disappeared months earlier after helping them with the case involving Jin, but Autumn had kept in touch.

> Sam the Spy: How's tricks?

> Autumn: Okay. Working with the new team.

> Sam the Spy: Why did they move you?

> Autumn: Not moved. Just training so we understand their mission.

> Sam the Spy: So, Sexy Seth is your team leader?

> Autumn: No.

> Sam the Spy: Yep. You guys make a cute couple.

She rolled her eyes and chuckled. Sam had been trying to get Autumn to hook up with Seth for months.

> Autumn: Got other things going on. There's a new synthetic on the streets.

Sam, God bless her, immediately understood what that meant.

> Sam the Spy: Joseph back in business?

> Autumn: Appears to be.

> Sam the Spy: Send me the info, and I'll start digging.

Hacking is what she meant. Autumn knew Sam had been a CIA white hat hacker in another lifetime before having to go on the run.

> Autumn: Thanks. Was there another reason you texted?

> Sam the Spy: Naw. I just wanted to let you know that the preliminary interview with Jin is excellent.

She did a lot of work for Jin as a quasi-PA.

> Autumn: Thanks.

> Sam the Spy: NP. Also, heads up, I might be hard to get hold of. I might have to ditch this number.

She had been on the run for years, and this was a common occurrence.

> Autumn: Trouble?

> Sam the Spy: Not sure, but just be aware, I might disappear for a week or two. Told Jin already. Be safe and take some time to play with Sexy Seth.

"Ready?"

She blinked and looked up. The man in question was standing in her doorway. Gah, this man.

"Yeah."

She grabbed her gun and badge and then followed him out the door.

"I thought you could ride with me."

She frowned. "Why?"

"I want to review what we will concentrate on for the training mission."

"Okay."

She followed him to the common room where the rest of Team Bravo had gathered. Everyone turned to look at them as they joined the team. Expressions ranged from mildly interested to speculative to downright giddy. That last one was Nikki.

"We'll go over to use the training area close to Kaneohe. Weather should be good today."

"Are we taking the van?"

They had a van for the team, but Seth shook his head. "It's getting the tires replaced today. Y'all ride with Ryan and Maya."

A beat of silence filled the room, and all of a sudden, she realized what Seth had done. The two of them would be together in a car for at least a thirty-minute drive, depending on the traffic. As Ian said all the time, bollocks.

"Let's get going," Seth said, apparently unaware that his team was tossing speculative looks their way. She didn't say anything but followed him out to his SUV. All team leaders had an issued SUV.

"Isn't this a waste?"

He unlocked the doors and waited until they were inside before engaging.

"What do you mean?"

She put on her seatbelt and then looked over at him. He had no idea what she was talking about.

"Seth, your people think you got me alone for a reason."

He blinked, those amazing long lashes captivating her momentarily and making her lose her train of thought.

"They do not."

"You are not *this* dense. They think you wanted to talk to me."

He shook his head, then turned to start his SUV. "Of course, they know I want to talk to you. I want to go over some things about today's training."

She said nothing, trying to decide if he was just messing with her. She decided he might be obtuse as he pulled out onto Ala Moana.

"Listen, SEAL, your people think there's a vibe between us."

"A vibe?"

He was so calm, as if nothing significant was happening. The truth was, typically, she didn't care. Her private life was just that, private. But this was work, and for the first time, she'd found a place where she belonged, with people she cared about. Besides Sam and Ian, she had never really worried about what people thought of her. Now, she did.

"You know what I mean."

He pulled to a stop at a light. "No. I don't."

She growled, and he laughed.

"What?" she demanded.

"You." He looked at her, his mouth turned up in that stupid crooked smile, and she found her entire body reacting. "I get it, Bradford. We're attracted to each other."

She crossed her arms beneath her breasts and looked out the windshield. "If you say so."

Seth snorted. "Yeah, I do." The light turned green. "I just don't know what to do about it now."

"Oh, you don't know what to do with me. I mean, I didn't know you were a virgin."

"Well, I know I would like to take you back to my place, strip you down, and spend enough time with my head between your legs that you forget your first and last names."

That caused images to flood her brain of how good it would be. Her nipples hardened, her panties were damp, and he hadn't even touched her. He was lethal.

To protect herself, she sniffed. "That's if I would ever let you."

"Oh, you would. You're imagining it right now."

Because she was, and because she didn't trust her voice, she said nothing.

"I just haven't decided if it would be good."

"Now you're admitting you suck at sex."

"No. We both have a lot on our plates and while I think we would be outstanding together in bed, I'm not sure you want that or if you're interested in a relationship." She glanced at him as he took the exit for H-3. He shrugged. "What can I say? I'm a monogamous kind of guy. I'm too old to play around at work just for funsies."

She wanted to mock him, but for some reason, that comment had her heartwarming.

"But for now, I want to talk about the mission today. We'll worry about the other stuff later."

She didn't respond. She couldn't. Usually, she wouldn't like his tone, but today, she shoved her irritation and most of her attraction to the back of her mind.

"Okay, hit me up."

six

A COUPLE DAYS LATER, Seth worried he had made a colossal mistake telling her how he felt. He had to follow orders, but Del and Adam had asked his opinion on how to get the teams integrated. He knew that Alpha didn't completely understand their mission. So he had opened his stupid mouth and suggested this.

Granted, he hadn't expected Autumn to be the first Team Alpha member to join them. She always seemed to have so much going on. When Adam mentioned it early Monday morning, he had caught Seth by surprise. He thought for sure Marcus would have been the first Alpha member to train with them. If it hadn't been for some foreign dignitary hitting Oahu in the next twenty-four hours, Marcus would be too busy. His terrorism background helped with any kind of attack that might happen.

Autumn worked hard that he would give her, but she had been right. She had needed to work on her upper body. As he trudged into the bullpen, he realized his body was already vibrating with that strange energy he always seemed to have around her. There was something just off about his feelings towards her. He couldn't figure it out.

All of the team was there except Autumn. He felt deflated when he noticed she wasn't in the room.

"Don't worry, Harry. She's just talking to Del and Adam about something on that drug bust," Tamilya said.

He glanced over and saw Autumn talking to her boss and Del, and she did not look happy. The fact that she was here and that she would go out with them had his heart singing. Okay, that was weird. Why would he be that happy about the woman who vexed him every chance she got? The day before, she had messed with his head on purpose while they had been grappling, and he still hadn't been able to move on from it.

Her frown turned darker as she started arguing with Del about something.

"Hey," Tamilya said, stepping closer. "Chill out, dude."

He glanced at his ex-girlfriend. They had dated when both of them had been in a dark place. They put the pieces of their lives back together. Now, they were just good friends.

"What?"

She glanced down at his hands. It was then that he realized he'd curled his fingers into fists. He forced himself to calm down. Again, it was a weird reaction. Autumn Bradford didn't want or need him fighting her battles. He had never known a woman as independent as Autumn Bradford.

"She's just pissed there's another delay in a trial. She's the arresting officer, and I know she worked her ass off on it. So, let's talk about your reaction."

"What?" Seth asked as he walked to his office. He needed a moment away from prying eyes. Tamilya followed him.

After she shut the door—without asking if he had time to chat—she sat in front of his desk.

"What's going on with you?"

"There's nothing going on with me." Lies. He was telling so many lies this week to other people and to himself.

She snorted. "You are wound tighter than when you were on Teams."

Probably because a woman who smelled like sunshine and temptation wasn't on his SEAL team. That would have been disastrous. He said nothing as he continued to ignore her. Unfortunately, Tamilya knew him too well.

"Oh...oh!" He looked up. "You have a thing for Autumn."

"I do not."

She snorted again. "Yeah, I get it now. Having her on the team while you have the hots for her has got to be hard. In more ways than one."

Then she giggled at her joke. Of course, it was funny for her. She had her happily ever after, a good man in Marcus. Was she the one getting off to the image of her teammate while in the shower this morning? No. And sadly, it was the hardest orgasm in a vey long time and ultimately unsatisfying. He was worried about the reason for that.

"Fine, I'll stop messing with you."

"Thank you."

"Since I'm not the one you want to mess around with."

"Like you would want that with Marcus in your life."

And not for the first time, a goofy smile curved her lips. Yeah, that was getting irritating. Not that she was happy. If someone deserved happiness, it was Tamilya. Simply put, he wanted that for himself. He had never thought about it, but it had been front and center for the last few months.

"And I have a meeting out at Pearl Harbor-Hickam. Marcus is doing some interviews so I'm filling in. Have fun."

"Sure. Fun."

She laughed and stepped out of his office, shutting the door behind her. He had work to do before they started their training session, so he pushed aside thoughts of Autumn Bradford and got to work. Of course, life had been handing him grenades lately, so he wasn't surprised when she knocked at the door and didn't wait for him to tell her to come in.

Without a word, she shut the door and sat down. She was vibrating with anger.

"Was there something you wanted?"

She hesitated. "I was wondering if I could beg off training today."

He sat back in his chair and studied her. "Was there something you needed to do?"

"I need not to be near people. That's what I need."

It was such a definitive statement as if she was barely holding on to her temper. "Do you want to explain why?"

"No."

He chuckled, and her eyes narrowed as she stared at him. He held up his hands. "Sorry. I'm not used to having people respond with such blatant animosity."

"It isn't animosity. It's the truth."

There was something beneath the surface. There always was with Autumn. She hid so much from everyone. Did she hide it from Ian, too? From the man she called her father? It seemed that Autumn hid a little of something from everyone, and that wasn't good for anyone—especially in a job that had high suicide rates.

"Of course, but no."

"What?"

"I understand you're being truthful, but you should train with us today. I assume that's what Del and Adam told you when you talked to them?"

She crossed her arms beneath her breasts and gave him a death stare. "No comment."

He let the moment of silence stretch out as they studied each other. Autumn was vibrating with some kind of energy. He knew part of it was irritation, but she was wound so tight. Seth had a feeling that with one little argument, she would lose her barely controlled anger.

She needed to get out of there, and he needed her not to get her ass in trouble. He didn't know why, but for some reason, he wanted to protect her from herself.

"Tell you what, I'll have Rami lead the briefings this morning. Most of it is about Maui, which you don't need since you lived there at one time. And let's be honest, very rarely will you go over there to help out. We'll be working with local law enforcement and the military."

"Cool story, bro."

The snark in her voice made him chuckle. Typically, if someone talked to him like that at work, he would smack them down for it. But she was different. She wasn't in his chain of command, and she made him laugh with that tone.

"We'll go out."

"What? Why?"

Was that panic in her voice? "I want to get to know you better for team cohesion. Also, you probably know a few things about the islands, especially Maui, that could help in our training."

She didn't say anything for a long moment. "I haven't been back since I left."

"I'm trying to give you an out today. Work with me here, Bradford."

"I don't want to be around you."

He would like to say that it didn't hurt hearing the words, but it did. He knew she was attracted to him but didn't particularly like him. He had laid out his thoughts the other day, but she hadn't told him as much as he had told her. "So, it's me that's irritating you?"

She sighed. "No. People. I don't want to be around people."

That was definitely true from her tone, but Seth knew of one thing that would get her out the door.

"How about we go have a snack—my treat. We don't have to talk."

She cocked her head to one side. "What are you up to, SEAL?"

He held his hands up again. "Nothing. Just giving you an option to do this rather than ignore a direct order from your team leader and Del."

She sighed, and he knew he had won the argument. He didn't pump his fist, but he wanted to. "Fine, but I expect food. Don't pull an Ian."

That guy. He knew she saw him as her brother, but it annoyed Seth when the guy's name was mentioned. "What's an *Ian*?"

"He lures me out of the office for food, then we end up at his place, and I have to cook."

"You can cook?"

She held up her finger and wagged it back and forth at him.

"Nope. Not falling for it. You have ten minutes, or I'm bailing on my own."

And then, with that, she left him alone. She was definitely a little more relaxed, knowing that she was getting out of the office. Seth was sure it had more to do with her needing space and less about that case or even him.

One thing was for sure, if he didn't make it out there in ten minutes, Autumn would leave him. He grabbed his gun and headed out into the bullpen. With a motion with his head, he got Rami to join him.

"I need you to handle the Maui discussion this morning."

They were set to review some of Maui's known local gang affiliations.

"Okay, any particular reason?"

"Remember that time you needed a break from training a month back?"

Rami's PTSD made him hyper-aware. He had it under control most of the time, but he'd had a bad episode last month. Seth had picked up on it and ordered him out of the office. Getting outside could sometimes give Rami relief from his PTSD symptoms.

"Ah, okay." He leaned closer. "Do you think she has PTSD?"

He had never thought about it before, but going over what little he knew, there was a chance she did.

"Not sure, but the boss ordered her to work with us today. Since we have a briefing, she doesn't need to go over it with us, so I thought it best to get her out of the office."

Rami nodded and said nothing. Maybe he was speculating just like the others on the team. Seth wasn't an idiot. Everyone here was in each other's business. But he did not want anything to blow back on Autumn.

"Gotcha."

"You're in charge."

He didn't say anything to anyone else. One thing he liked about TFH is that while it was run like a combat unit in many ways, there was more freedom. Del wouldn't question where he was. He found her pacing by his SUV. There was something about that pacing, the way her hips swung, and the underlying sensuality to her movements that always got to him. She did a lot of pacing in the common area, her office, and all over the place. She never seemed to be able to hold still."

"Let's go. Where do you want to eat?"

She said nothing until they were both in his vehicle. "Let's go to Anna Miller's."

The local place was in Aiea, about twenty to thirty minutes away, depending on the traffic.

"You got it."

"And I don't want to talk about things."

"Fine," he said, trying to hide his smile. He knew that was a lie. He could be patient.

They were seated by the window with a view of the parking lot. In Hawaii, even parking lots were pretty, in her opinion.

Anna Miller's was on the top floor of two restaurants. Down below was another of her favorites, Bravo's. She would cut a bitch if they got in her way of those garlic rolls. They had a view of the morning traffic and the watercress farm.

"What's good here?"

She looked up from her menu. "You've never been here?"

He shook his head. "I'm still checking out places."

"Ah. Do you like pancakes?"

"Of course, I like pancakes. I'm not a monster."

She smiled. "I suggest one of their banana Mac nut pancakes. They don't have them every morning, but they do today, so I suggest those."

Both of them ordered the pancakes and coffee. Once they were alone, Autumn studied him. "Want to tell me why you sprung me?"

"That's an odd phrase. I thought you liked work."

"I do." She sighed. "Just sometimes, I have to get out. When I'm investigating, that's easier. What y'all do is a lot of training."

"Have you ever talked to a therapist?"

She blinked. It was such a sudden topic switch.

"Yep, lots of them. After getting out of Joyous Wave and after a couple of missions while in the DEA, I know what's wrong with me. I usually have a handle on it, but it's been a little difficult lately."

The waitress returned with their coffees. Once they were alone, Seth seemed to wait for her to speak again. Interesting. She liked patience in a man.

"I've had some issues since we took down Hank."

He nodded. "You really didn't like him."

Hank Seymour had been in Joseph's inner circle. All the bad memories intensified when he popped up a few months ago.

"You mean my betrothed?"

He made a face of disgust, and she couldn't help but laugh. "Yeah. Imagine my feelings being sixteen when Joseph said I would marry him within a month. So, yeah, I have issues, and most of the time, they're under control."

"But you've been stuck with us."

"I wouldn't call it that, SEAL. I would call it more of being on someone else's schedule."

"I'm sorry, I don't see the difference."

She sat back and toyed with her coffee cup. "I bet you have some great childhood memories. Playing with your brothers or just hanging out."

"Yeah."

"I don't. My memories consist of work. Everyone had a job at Joyous Wave except the old creeps—and I include Joseph Watters in that category—had something they had to do. There was a reason I didn't know how to handle a computer or a phone. Even a landline was odd to me when I escaped. So, when I have to do things day in and day out on someone else's schedule, I have minor freakouts."

"You should talk to Adam about it."

"No."

The waitress returned with their pancakes. One of the things Autumn loved about Anna Miller's was how fast their cooks were.

Once their coffees were topped off and they were left alone once again, Seth continued with the discussion. Because, of course, he did.

"Why not? It isn't something to be ashamed of."

She chewed on her banana Mac nut pancake, loving the hit of sweetness and the yummy nuts.

"I'm not ashamed. I just know how to deal with it."

"Bottling it up and getting angry at your boss is not how to deal with it."

"That's rude."

"Well, so are you."

There was a beat of silence as she watched him dig into his plate of pancakes like he was going to war. The truth of the comment sent a wave of humor slicing through her irritation. Giggles bubbled up and then exploded out of her. When he looked up at her, his eyes were dancing.

"That's a nice sound, Bradford."

"What? I laugh a lot."

"No. Not like that. That was joy. You should do it more often."

She sighed. "Yeah, well, sometimes it's hard."

"I get it. I deal with my own issues. Actually, both of my brothers do, too."

"They're military?"

He nodded as he shoved another piece of pancake into his mouth. Once he chewed it, he said, "Gus is in the Marines, and Bennett's the weird one. He went into the Air Force."

"How is that weird?"

"We're a Navy family."

"Apparently not. And while technically the Marine Corps is under the Navy, it's not the same. And let me guess about Bennett. He wanted to fly."

"Yes, like he couldn't do that in the Navy, or at least, the plane he wanted."

"What's he fly?"

"That's not important."

"Not a fighter because those are in other services. Being a helicopter pilot...the best way to move up in rank and be an officer is in the Air Force. Let me guess on that, too. He's with a rescue squad."

"Yes."

She smiled.

"And your parents are coming here?"

"Yeah, my brothers are still in the military and moving around. Your father's moving here because you and Ian are here."

She nodded. "He had to have a kidney transplant last year. Thankfully, a close relative was a match, so he didn't have to go on the register."

"And he couldn't stay there."

She shook her head, her thoughts returning to how MI-6 wouldn't take no for an answer.

"His old bosses would call him in to consult. And Sam, being who he is, wouldn't tell them no. When Ian was there, he could keep them at bay, but once he moved here, they would call Sam all the time. His health is good, but the stress isn't good on him, so Ian convinced him to move here."

He nodded. It didn't take long to finish her pancakes and order a slice of pie. Once they were back on the road, she turned to face Seth.

"Thanks."

"You're welcome. Just tell people you need a break. They won't think less of you."

She knew he was right, but the truth was, everything was coming to a head. Things were moving along. Joseph was out there circling her, waiting for her to slip up. Autumn knew that the two of them would end up facing each other, and everything would change. As long as Joseph went down, that was all that mattered.

"Autumn?"

She blinked when she realized she had been staring at him like a goober. "Sorry. And yes, I will."

He smiled, apparently satisfied with her comment. God, he was pretty. And in that one moment, she wished she were an ordinary woman. She would love to go on dates and have a relationship. Never before had she yearned for those ordinary things, but this man, with his quiet ways and easy smiles, had her thinking just how wonderful they would be.

But her life wasn't her own, and fantasizing about what could be was a waste of time.

seven

BY FRIDAY, Autumn was still a little sore. She hadn't worked on her upper body that much, and she understood now what a mistake that was. She had always concentrated on her cardio. Running and swimming. Swimming helped her arms a little bit, but they had not been prepared for the exercises they ran for carrying dead weight. Ugh.

Plus, she had to work with Seth in a few grappling sessions. The man was...okay, solid, clever, and hot AF—as the big boss said these days. Even as exhausted as she was, she hadn't been sleeping well. Thankfully, this was the last day with Bravo. Monday, she would be back on Team Alpha. She would miss spending as much time with Seth's team, but she was ready for a break. She trudged up the stairs to her apartment, ready for a hot shower and food. That's when she realized she hadn't shopped for food. Dammit.

"Hey, pretty Autumn," Freddy called out. She stepped on the shared landing for their apartments.

"Hey, how are you doing?"

He shook his head. "Can't complain. You look like a dead dog."

"You see dead dogs walking around?"

He smiled, revealing those three missing teeth. Autumn's heart hurt for him. A lifetime of addiction had left him with no family or real friends. His health was diminishing more and more each day.

"Not ones as pretty as you."

It wasn't a come-on at all. It was the way she thought a grandfather would say it to his granddaughter. She had no idea since she had never met her grandfathers, thanks to Joseph.

"You're sweet. I just started a new workout, and I'm getting my ass kicked."

He nodded.

"Did you have something for me?"

"Not yet. Soon, though. I'm sure of it."

"Just be careful."

"I will. Hope you feel better."

He disappeared back into his apartment, shutting the door quietly. Autumn realized there was a good chance that Freddy would probably go for days without human contact if she didn't talk to him. That wasn't a good thing.

Her phone vibrated in her pocket before she could get through her door.

> Ian: Twenty minutes out.

> Ian: Please tell me you remembered Dad was getting here today.

> Autumn: I remembered.

She didn't. She'd been so hot and bothered by her time in Seth's realm that she was losing track of important things.

She had exactly twenty minutes to shower and get dressed. There was no way she could let Sam down. She owed that man her life.

After a five-minute shower, she dried her hair, leaving it slightly damp. It would kink up, but her father wouldn't care. Looking at her clothes, she almost grabbed a pair of her cargo pants but decided against it. She felt like a sun dress was in order. Grabbing her favorite green maxi sundress, she slipped it on. It was simple, but the fabric clung to her meager curves, dipping low in the front. It brought out the green in her eyes. She never wore much makeup but felt she needed a little tonight.

After slipping on her mother's locket, she checked herself in the mirror and smiled. Her phone buzzed.

> Ian: Tell me you're ready.

She didn't answer because she knew it would irritate him. After donning her sandals, she stepped out of the apartment. Ian was sitting in an SUV. More than likely, it was one from Dillon Security. The window tint was just on this side of legal in Hawaii. The truth was, she knew Ian hated SUVs. He tended to drive sports cars. Spies. They always thought they were cooler than the rest of them.

Once she climbed into the SUV, she connected her phone and played music. Ian said nothing but rolled his eyes. He was silent as he backed out of the parking space. She knew it drove him crazy. Ian loved to be in control of things almost as much as she did. Therefore, she was a master of figuring out what bothered him the most. He really did not love Hawaiian music the way she did.

"You forgot."

"I did not." Lies. She was good at them. Always had been.

"You did, but I can understand since you're so wrapped up in your time with the pretty boy."

"What do you mean by that?"

He shrugged as he eased onto H-1 to head to the airport.

"Why would you call Harrington a pretty boy?" He definitely wasn't a boy.

"Interesting that you picked up on exactly who I was talking about."

"Shut it."

He didn't say anything, but he smiled. *Ugh.* Brothers. She turned up the music and started singing just to annoy him. She couldn't carry a tune to save her life. In fact, there was a good chance she could crack glass with how bad she sang. And Ian, who had an amazing tenor voice, always got irritated when she sang off-key, especially pop music. He was a snob.

Thanks to the traffic, it took them about twenty minutes to get to the airport.

"We need a lei."

"No, we don't."

"Yes, we do. Stop so I can buy one. Dad's plane just landed. He won't be at baggage claim for at least ten minutes."

He sighed while he took the exit for the lei stand. Lei makers rented out stands for people to buy leis for those coming to the islands. She was picking out a very pretty Ti-leaf lei when someone stepped up beside her.

It was odd that she didn't hear anyone since her senses were usually on alert, but that was because Ian had been watching out for her. When she turned, she fought the urge to take a step back. Standing next to her was Seth Harrington. She couldn't get away from the man.

"What are you doing here?"

"Looking to buy a gun."

She snorted. "No, why would you be at a lei stand?"

"My parents are getting here, or they just arrived."

Their parents had been on the same plane?

"And you?"

"Our father."

"Our?"

She pointed to a very irritated Ian, who was watching the by-play. He drummed the steering wheel with his fingers.

"Oh, I didn't notice him."

She wanted to laugh at Seth's irritated tone. The woman came over so Autumn could pay for the lei.

"Hmm."

He should not make that noise in public. Not near her, at least. It sent little waves of heat coursing through her blood. "What?"

"I don't know which one to get."

"Well," she said, holding up her lei, "this is the best one for guys, but your mom, what's her favorite color?"

"Blue. It was always all over the house. We even had a blue house one time."

She snorted again.

"There you go. Get her one with blue flowers. See ya later," she said, practically running away. She wasn't proud of it. Once she climbed back into the SUV, her brother smirked as he backed out of the parking spot.

"Your boy has a crush."

Butterflies filled her belly, and she frowned. "What do you mean?"

He said nothing as he drove around to the parking lot. Autumn knew this was one of his ploys, so she tried to control her need to demand an answer. He was such a butthead. Spies... they always liked to control the narrative even if they weren't in the business anymore.

He parked his car, and she still said nothing, even though she wanted to scream at him. She should be used to this, but while they weren't raised together, they were siblings. He knew exactly how to get under her skin.

Finally, as they stood at the crosswalk waiting for the traffic to pass, he said, "Harrington was checking you out."

Again, those butterflies took flight but were more like drunken butterflies. They were making Autumn feel a little sick to her stomach.

"He was not."

It was so insane that she simultaneously wanted it to be true and false. And yes, a few days ago, he'd told her he wanted her, but it still did nothing to calm her nerves.

She glanced at Ian. That stupid smirk sent her temper soaring. She hated these kinds of games, and they had less to do with Ian than her time at Joyous Wave. The mind fuck they seemed to get off on there was enough to make any average person insane. She always thought it was a good thing that she wasn't normal.

"He was. The few times I've seen you two in the same room, there's a buzz."

The light changed, allowing them to cross, but it took her a second to move. She was long-legged for her height, but Ian was a giant. She hurried to catch up with him. The automatic doors opened, the rush of air hit her, and she shivered. The Honolulu Airport was packed, but that was the norm. Several mainland flights always seemed to hit in the late afternoon.

The moment she saw Sam, her heart jumped. He looked so much better than he had a few months ago. Retiring had definitely been good for him. His color was good, and he now donned a full beard.

Ignoring Ian, she rushed forward, jumping into Sam's arms. He was the first man she had ever learned to trust, and almost losing him this year freaked her out. The kidney transplant was doing well, but she always worried something would go wrong.

He smelled familiar, that same bergamot and spice that always seemed to cling to him.

She saw Seth approach a handsome couple out of the corner of her eye. Jesus, his father, looked just like him but had twenty to twenty-five more years on him. His mother was tall, with short, ash-blonde hair, and dressed smartly in a blue shirt tucked into jeans. She was wearing tennis shoes. Also, she did not have a hair out of place and not one wrinkle in her clothes. She had just spent at least six hours on a flight and looked like a million bucks.

"Do you know them?" Sam asked.

"No. But I know their son."

"Ah. Yes, I talked to them on the plane. Let's go meet them."

"Let's not and say we did."

Ian chuckled. "She doesn't want to go because she has a crush on Seth."

"I do not." And now she sounded defensive. Brothers were the worst. "Fine, let's go."

They made their way over to the Harringtons.

"Oh, there you are," his mother said. She and Seth shared the same eyes. "I guess our kids *do* work together."

The coincidence would make her skin itch, but the truth was, there was no odd reason behind their parents being on the same plane. There were only so many flights from the mainland each day.

Sam pulled her closer. "This is Autumn, and this is my son Ian. This is Thelma and Dennis Harrington."

Ian, being the ultimate player, put Sam's cases down, took Mrs. Harrington's hand, and held it between the two of his.

"It is such a pleasure to meet you. Although, I'm having a hard time believing you are old enough to have a son the age of Harry over there."

The giggle did not sound like something that would come out of a woman like Thelma Harrington. The woman was a powerhouse and had been one of the most powerful women at the Pentagon. From the look on Seth's face, he wasn't used to it, either.

"Of course, you know him. Sam, this is my oldest son, Seth."

Sam shook Seth's hand. "Nice to meet you. I gather Autumn's been training with you lately."

"Today was the last day," she said.

Seth laughed. "Oh, yeah, she had a ball with us. She complained every day."

"I did not. I had some things I needed to do."

"Sure, you did."

"It's just like you to think that I have nothing else to do other than to follow y'all around all over the place and train in the gym."

They both noticed that both their families watched them with interest.

"Yes, I have some work to do next week, and I understand their mission now. I heard you're getting Graeme next week." She looked at Thelma. "He's our Thor. You'll meet him tomorrow night."

"Tomorrow night?" Thelma asked.

"Oh." She looked at Seth and blinked a few times, trying to look innocent. "You *did* tell your mother about the party at Mrs. Lee's house, right?"

"No, he did not." That tone told her she had just gotten him in trouble with his mother. It made her smile.

"I was going to tell you once you got in. See how you felt."

"Well, it's tomorrow night, and her fried rice is to die for. Plus, Drew's family—he's another member of Team Alpha—is catering a lot of it along with the aunties."

"Sounds like a great time," his father said.

"Well, we'll see you there."

As they headed out the door, Sam asked, "How long have you and that Harrington been dating?"

"I'm not dating him."

"He definitely wants to date her," Ian offered.

"He does not." And again, she was sounding defensive.

"I told you he was checking you out."

"That doesn't mean he wants to date me."

"What the hell does it mean?" Sam asked.

"He probably just wants to bang me."

Her father sighed. "I really regret telling both of you to speak freely when you were in your teens."

Life was good—at least for the moment. And she had

learned that living in the moment was more important than anything else.

———

Seth took the ramp that led to H-1 and knew it was just a matter of time before his mother said something. They were staying in Honolulu while they waited for their household goods to arrive. Still, he knew the quick twenty-minute drive to their rented condo wouldn't be fast enough to outrun his mother.

"Autumn seems interesting."

His father chuckled from the back seat, but Seth knew he would be no help. He might be a retired admiral, but he knew better than to tangle with his wife.

"She is."

"From how you talked about her, I thought she was kind of tomboyish."

He knew where she was going with this. "Is that a term you should use now? I don't think it is."

"What I meant was that you talked about the way she fought and that she had a great record with drug busts. You didn't say anything about her being stunning."

"It's the first time I've ever seen her in a dress."

"Oh. Then you didn't know she was so pretty?"

He rolled his eyes. "Of course, I knew she was pretty."

"So you think she's attractive." Not a question, and he knew that his mother had backed him into a corner. He knew his father wasn't the only admiral with a healthy respect for his mother. Seth had to go on the offensive, or his mother would start meddling. She wasn't the typical mom who would just urge him to date. No, his mother had the type of contacts that would have an entire background check on someone within an hour.

"Anyone with eyes can see she's attractive."

There, that should work. The only thing that worried Seth was the chuckle from his father in the back seat.

"Indeed. That was her father and brother?"

As if he hadn't just introduced them back at the airport. "Why do you ask?"

She sighed.

Alarm coursed through him. "What did you do?"

"Nothing. I promise. I would have recognized her even if you didn't mention her background. Or at least, I recognize her because of her mother."

"You knew her mother?"

"No, not personally. When the standoff happened, her face was everywhere because of her father."

He hated it when his mother spoke in riddles. He had always been someone who wanted all the facts and no subterfuge. That made him pause as he slowed down for a red light. Is that why he was so intrigued by Autumn? He wanted to know the whole truth about what was happening with her.

"What about her grandfather?"

"Her grandfather was Arlen Bradford."

He blinked and glanced at his mother. "The Arlen Bradford of Bradford Industries?"

She nodded. "A lot of fuss was made about her mother. They were comparing her to Patty Hearst."

"Except she wasn't kidnapped like Hearst," his father said from the backseat.

"Agreed and Hearst definitely didn't have a baby with the

leader of that cult. Anyway, she looks a lot like her mother. Not as thin, that's for sure, but she is the spitting image of her mother."

Someone laid on their horn behind him, and he realized the light had turned green.

"So, you think she looks like her mother, and that's how you recognized her?"

"Don't sound so suspicious. And yes. If you looked up Autumn's mother, you would see it. Anyways, she's a gorgeous woman."

"Yes, she is."

"Hmm, so you agree. Good."

Inwardly, he sighed. He now understood what Rami had been talking about and knew he would eat his words if his friend ever found out.

eight

AUTUMN WAS RUNNING LATE AGAIN. It was nothing new for her. Many people thought she was early to work because she was a workaholic. That wasn't the reason. Well, that wasn't the entire reason she showed up early. She *was* a workaholic. She had her regular caseload, and then she had her investigation into Joseph's shenanigans.

Yes, it was an unserious word for some very serious behavior. Still, it helped Autumn deal with the horror of the monster who "raised" her.

Anyway, she couldn't be late tonight. She'd had a few things to wrap up at work on her last case. Saturday was a great day to do paperwork. She paused in applying her blush.

What the hell, Bradford?

Yep, she needed to get out more. She had always had a work ethic, but never like this. And since she wasn't sure how much more time she had, she should be grabbing onto life with both hands. Instead, she had been getting deeper into what Joseph had been up to since he "died" and losing all perspective.

So, tonight, she would try. She would set her thoughts

about Joseph aside and celebrate two people who truly deserved their happily ever after.

Stepping back from the mirror, Autumn took in her dress. As she had told Nikki, she did own dresses. This one was another of her favorites. The white halter dress looked simple. The gauzy material floated around her and reached her ankles. But it cut deep between her breasts, making it impossible to wear a bra. The back was completely open.

After putting on a pair of simple diamond studs Ian had given her for Christmas last year, she found her sandals. This would be held in Merri's backyard, so there was no reason to wear heels.

The last bit was to pull her hair into a chignon to keep it off her neck. It was humid tonight, and the trade winds weren't expected to return for a few days. As she stepped out onto her landing, her phone buzzed.

> Ian: You are running late, right?

She rolled her eyes. Since her father was staying at the house she'd purchased, she had told them she would pick them up. Driving into Honolulu and then back to the Lee house made no sense.

> Autumn: On my way. Do you have the directions to the house?

> Ian: Of course.

She slipped her phone into her pocket and shut the door just as Freddy's door opened.

"Hey, pretty Autumn. You look amazing."

She smiled at him. "Thank you. Bossman is having a party for his engagement."

He nodded. "You know..." His voice trailed off, and he shook his head.

"What?"

He drew in a deep breath and looked up at her. "You look like your mother."

Alarm hit her first, winding its way through her entire body before she could stop it. It was her first reaction any time she ran into one of the former cult members. They were sometimes angry at her, thinking it was her fault that Joseph had a standoff with the feds. The truth was, they had been investigating him for months if not years.

Anger surged. She worried about this man and took care of him. Yes, he was definitely an informant, but he would have been dead if it hadn't been for her.

Freddy's creased face showed his regret as he held up his hands.

"No, don't worry. I'm not still a *True Believer*. I was at Joyous Wave until about a month before everything went to shit. I overdosed, and once the hospital got hold of me, my family found out and came to get me."

She was still on edge. Many of the survivors who claimed to be the true believers of Joseph Watters looked to her to be the next great leader. They thought that she would call them for the next great gathering. That was going to happen right after JFK Jr was elected president.

Worse, if they knew she'd hunted Joseph and plotted to send him straight to hell as soon as she could get hold of him, they would probably burn her alive.

He sighed. "I don't blame you for not believing me. I didn't pick up on it at first. I was having issues when you moved in."

Oh, yeah, he'd had several overdoses the first year she lived in the apartment next to his. He was still a drug addict, but he seemed to be functioning at the moment.

"Yes. I remember."

Her phone buzzed in her pocket, but she ignored it.

"She was always kind to a stupid boy like me."

"You aren't stupid."

"I'm not that boy anymore."

And more than likely, his drug addiction started at Joyous Wave.

"I felt bad for not telling you."

She nodded. "Well, thanks."

"I also wanted to tell you that I'm hot on the trail of the person moving the new synthetic. They're calling it The Rapture."

Her heartbeat almost tripled in just a few seconds. "The Rapture?"

He nodded. That was definitely Joseph. He was such a nut job. He probably really loved that name because he knew there would be true believers he could sell to. And now, if Joseph remembered Freddy, he was in more danger. Joseph wouldn't hesitate killing Freddy to prove a point, especially if he was worried Freddy would tell people he was still alive.

"Don't worry about finding the person in charge."

He frowned. "That's what I do for you."

"No, just getting the name is great. It will be easy to run down. I'll get the money to you by Monday, okay?"

He didn't look like he was convinced. Worry crept through Autumn. She still wasn't happy that he hadn't been honest with her. While she fudged the truth from time to time, she hated liars. Being "raised" by a pathological liar tended to do that to you. But...she would be devastated if anything happened to him because of her investigation.

"Promise me."

He sighed and then nodded.

"Do you still have that gift card?"

"Yes."

"Go get something to eat. I'd join you, but as I said, this is for the bossman and his fiancé."

He nodded, then his lips curved. "You have a good time, Autumn. I'll see you later."

As she watched him shuffle back into his apartment, a sense of foreboding took over her. She wanted to demand that he go eat right now, but she understood addicts. He would go if he felt like it, but there was a good chance he would get high tonight.

Was she getting bad vibes about an overdose, or was it something different? With a shake of her head, she pushed the worries out of her mind. Autumn knew that he would keep his promise to her.

———

Seth rolled his shoulders as he watched his parents mingling with his workmates. It was the first time he'd ever brought them to something like this. His parents had been to his promotions and retirement but never really mingled like this. It was surreal, and it made him a little antsy.

"What's wrong?" Rami asked. Seth glanced at the former SEAL.

"Why do you think there's something wrong?"

"You keep rolling your shoulders. It's your tell."

Nikki stepped up. The former Coastie had definitely understood the dress code. She was wearing a dress that stopped at mid-thigh. Not that he would ever have noticed, but Rami had complained about it when she'd shown up thirty minutes earlier.

"He's right. You've been surveying the area."

She sipped her Mai Tai.

"Hyper vigilance," Rami said.

"No. Someone is waiting for a certain someone to appear." She leaned closer and waved her drink. "She's over there."

For a second, he didn't look. He hadn't been able to get Autumn out of his head since yesterday—since he had met her. There was just something about her. At the moment, he felt like a teenager with his first real crush. Looking at her might make him pass out.

"That's not the problem," Rami said as Seth finally found Autumn in the crowd. She was introducing her father to Merri and a few of the aunties. She was wearing another dress made out of gauzy material. It shouldn't reduce him to babbling just because she wore something like a dress. It was just so different than what he was used to seeing her wear.

Then, she turned, and Seth lost all ability to think. The dress plunged low between her breasts, and there was no way she was wearing a bra.

Fuck.

Thankfully, years of training allowed him to control his emotions—*all* of them. He ordered his body to calm the fuck down. He wasn't some seventeen-year-old with a crush. Autumn laughed at something Adam said. It irritated him even though he knew there was no reason to worry about it. Adam was her boss and in love with Jin Phillips. In fact, the Alpha Team leader had waited years for Jin to recover from a horrific attack.

Then, Autumn turned her head. Their gazes connected, and, at that moment, it was like they were the only people there. The chatter and music faded, leaving him completely entranced with their connection. Of course, his mother stepped in his line of view, her hand outstretched to greet Autumn.

"Oh, your mom looks like she's checking out Autumn," Nikki said.

The entire crew had met his parents when they'd arrived at the party.

"They already met."

A whistle sounded beside him, and he realized that Kap and Ryan had joined them.

"So, your mom met her yesterday and then zeroed in on Autumn the moment she arrived."

"Yeah. I mean, she didn't zero in on her the moment she arrived." But she had, and that worried him. As he said, his mother wasn't one to pry into his social life. She seemed to be very interested in Autumn.

"I think your mom wants babies, and she thinks Autumn would be a great candidate," Kap said.

"What? No." But now that Kap mentioned it, he could imagine having Autumn in his life as more than a work colleague.

"Yeah, Kap," Nikki said. "It's not like someone with her background would be a good fit for marriage and two point five kids."

He was already irritated with his crew for speculating what

his mother was doing. Still, it turned to agitation on Autumn's behalf.

"What the hell do you mean by that?"

His crew stilled. He rarely lost his temper, and they had never seen it happen. They just hadn't been working together that long.

"There's always talk, Seth," Ryan said quietly.

"Well, there shouldn't be. Autumn might not be on our team, but she's on *the* team. And as a woman, I would think you would know better than to speculate, Nikki."

Again, silence greeted him. He knew he was making an ass out of himself, but Nikki should know better. Women in their business always had to deal with people equating their job to their sexuality. How many times did female law enforcement have to deal with handcuff jokes?

"Sorry, boss," Nikki said. "You're right."

He nodded and stepped away from them. He could feel all of them watching him. He took off in the opposite direction to prove to them and himself that he wasn't that infatuated with Autumn. He needed a moment to figure out why he got so pissed off at his crew. They had only been joking, although he did not like Nikki's assumptions. Was it because what she said was inappropriate, or did he want to be untrue? Why would he care if she wanted more than casual hookups?

Before he could work all that out, Del called out to him. Great. He probably wanted to ream him for what had happened. Seth hadn't raised his voice, but Del had a keen sense. As former special forces and now commander of TFH, he had to be aware.

"Hey, boss," he said.

"Everything okay with Bravo?"

He nodded. "Yeah. They were speculating, and it irritated me."

"Oh, okay. You mean about you and Autumn?"

He rolled his eyes. "Does everyone think there's something going on?"

"No. I don't actually give a fuck."

He blinked, then chuckled. "Then why did you just ask about it?"

"Listen, as long as it doesn't get in the way of work, I don't care. She doesn't directly work for you. And yeah, I know people, and I have seen how she reacts around you."

"What way?"

Del shook his head. "I'm not in high school. You figure that shit out. Also, be careful around Autumn."

"Are you warning me off her?"

"No. I know she has much more going on beneath the surface than most of us know."

"Even you?"

"Especially me. Also, she's...fragile."

He cocked his head to the side and studied his boss. "You're worried about her."

It was not a question because there was no denying the concern in his boss's voice.

"Yeah. She's been more on edge lately, but with Sam getting a transplant last year, she's been getting worse."

He filed that information away. "Okay. Anything else?"

"Yeah, I'm giving you Graeme to take out on a few runs next week. I know he has a military background, but I want him to understand our procedures just in case you need him to help."

"Now I know I'm in trouble."

Del chuckled as his attention snagged on something in the crowd. Seth followed his line of sight and saw Emma, Del's wife. The diminutive woman was a genius in game theory and programming and was as beautiful as she was brilliant. After over five years of marriage, they also seemed to still be infatuated with each other.

"Harry," she said, using his old nickname from the military, "how are you this evening?"

"Doing great."

She turned to her husband. "See. I was nice."

He hid his smile. She was probably on the spectrum and actually really sweet. Granted, she was a little awkward, but he found it refreshing that she could be so blunt—just like Autumn. That had him blinking and looking across the yard. She was in a discussion with his mother about something that had his mother laughing.

"Your mother seems to like Autumn."

He glanced at Emma. "How can you tell?"

"She's laughing. Are you two dating?"

Of course, she was trying to feel him out. "Boss, your wife's been betting."

She gasped. It was so dramatic that Seth knew he was right. Del hated the betting, or he said he did. The fact that his wife was placing bets would probably not go over well with him.

"I need another beer," he said. "Have fun with that."

Then he headed for another drink because no matter how much he wanted to figure out his feelings about Autumn, it wouldn't happen tonight.

nine

NEEDING A MOMENT TO HERSELF, Autumn excused herself, saying she needed to use the bathroom. Lord, Seth's mother was a demon interrogator. She wasn't sure what the older woman had done for the Pentagon, but Thelma must have been good at it.

She slipped through Merri Lee's house. She had been here more than a few times. She told everyone it was for the fried rice, but as she passed the family photos lining the walls, it was actually for that. They were normal. Granted, Adam losing his father when he was young hadn't been easy, but they had had each other. When she was in this house, it was easy to feel the love between the siblings and their mother.

She stopped at a photo of a very young Adam on his Police Academy graduation day. He was surrounded by family. It wasn't just his sisters and mother, but uncles, aunties, cousins—both blood and not.

"I didn't think you lurked in other people's houses."

She jumped at Merri's voice. It wasn't like her to miss someone sneaking up on her, but she always felt safe here.

"Not lurking, admiring," she said without turning around.

"Potato-pot*aa*to," she said.

Autumn chuckled. "I needed a break."

"And you can do that anytime at my house."

She would not cry. It was a sign of weakness. That was an unhealthy thought, but it was hard to beat out the training from birth.

"Thank you."

"And I know that Thelma was giving you the third degree. Any reason for that?"

The speculation in her voice made Autumn's stomach tighten. She couldn't want that. Not ever. Seth was sexy and funny and when he had taken her out to breakfast, she'd wanted more. That was saying a lot. Never in all the years that she had been hunting Joseph had she had those thoughts of wanting to spend time getting to know a man.

"No."

Merri sighed. "You can want more."

Now, it was her turn to sigh. When she turned to face the older woman, she had to look down. Adam was a giant—something he got from his father. His mother was a petite woman. She just seemed like a giant because of her larger-than-life character.

"I don't."

One eyebrow rose up.

"Merri." The warning was unmistakable.

"I know what you've said. You don't want a serious relationship."

"I don't." And if she told herself that enough times, she might just believe it.

"Maybe not before that man showed up. Of course, he's been watching you all night."

"He has not."

"He has. From the moment he knew you were here, he has been tracking you."

She didn't know how she felt about that. Again, she was feeling off if Merri had noticed Seth tracking her and Autumn hadn't.

"And I can see you're trying to figure this out, but you don't have to do that tonight."

"There's nothing to figure out."

"Autumn, you can lie to me all you want, but before long, lying to yourself will bite you in the bum."

She smiled, and then it faded. "I told you. I'm broken."

"You are not broken, and I have told you I will banish you from this house for a month if you continue to say that. I mean it."

"I'm not normal."

Merri shrugged, her dark eyes filled with understanding. "Normal is boring, but I'll leave you alone about it. Besides, I think I'll go flirt with Sam."

"Be careful."

"Are you warning me off of him?"

"Good God, no. You're both adults. Just, Adam will freak out a little."

She knew that Adam's mother hadn't really dated much since his father was killed in the line of duty.

"Oh, good. You know...that accent," she said, humming.

"Ick. I don't want to know about that."

Merri wrapped her arm around Autumn. "Come on, I know you didn't need to use the bathroom."

Seth hurried outside, his mind reeling at what he'd overheard. He knew she was attracted to him, but he had no idea Autumn thought she was broken. Why would she believe that? And just what the hell happened at the cult that made her feel that? He knew that cults fucked with people's psyche, but he had no idea just how badly it had messed her up.

He had followed her into the house, worried that his mother had been rude, not on purpose. His mother had one of those personalities that could not let things go. Once she'd zeroed in on a topic, she would dig until she felt satisfied. He always knew to avoid the house when she was trying out new recipes. She was a horrible cook but never failed to find a new recipe she wanted to perfect.

"There you are," the woman in question said as he stepped out on the deck. It took him back to sneaking into the house after making out with Trudy Abelson. There was nothing like having a mother who could track your every move on instinct alone.

"What's up?"

He tried to sound casual, but from the look on his mother's face, he knew he hadn't achieved his goals.

"We're going to call a ride share. Your father and I are just not as young as we used to be."

"It's hard to get used to the time change after you move to Hawaii."

That was the truth. He knew people who kept waking up at four in the morning even if they didn't have to be awake.

"Hey, why don't you take my car?"

"Are you sure? How will you get home?"

"I can get someone on the team to drop me off."

"Are you sure? What will you do for transportation?"

"I have my work SUV if I get called in to work." Which could always happen. They constantly had tourists getting lost, and it only took one bad storm or an injury to turn it into something that could end with death if not found soon enough.

"If you're sure?"

He nodded. "No problem. You sure you don't want me to show you around tomorrow?"

They had discussed it, but his mother said there was no rush.

She shook her head. "I think I just want to laze about tomorrow."

"No worries."

He kissed her cheek just as Autumn stepped onto the deck. As he straightened, he watched Autumn and Merri make their way over to them. His mother turned to look at what caught his attention.

"Oh, Merri, thank you so much for letting us join the celebration."

"Are you leaving?" Merri asked.

"Yes, Dennis and I are still adjusting to the time change."

"Of course. Let's make up a plate for you to take back. That way, you don't have to do much tomorrow."

As the two women left him with Autumn, he realized she was looking anywhere but at him.

"You look nice."

Her gaze zeroed in on him. His body reacted immediately.

"Thank you."

And she did. She was a beautiful woman, but tonight, there was something different about her.

"So, your mom is abandoning you?"

He chuckled. "Seems like it."

"Yeah, well, Merri told me she wanted to bang Sam."

He barked out a laugh, and she smiled. Not the one he was used to. This one showed her dimples, and her eyes danced with amusement.

"Not sure how Adam is going to take that," she said with a shrug. "Or Ian, for that matter. He's kind of persnickety about his father dating—as if he can talk."

It was that. The humor she found at Ian's expense. A normal, mundane thing, but it put her on the outside again. It was as if she weren't part of the family unit, even though Ian and Sam clearly saw her that way. That made him want to know more, to pull her into the fold and make her understand that people liked her for being her.

I'm broken.

Those two words still rattled around in his head...in his heart. Del was right. She had a lot going on beneath the surface. She was definitely up to something, from what he could tell. Beyond her work with Team Alpha, she was doing some other digging because she had always whispered conversations on the phone with Ian. But Del also hit on the fragility.

"Why are you looking at me like that?"

Because he'd just realized he might be falling for the woman, and he hadn't even kissed her.

"I'm trying to figure out how to convince you to give me a ride back to my place tonight."

She tilted her head and studied him. "You're in luck because Sam and Ian came in Ian's car."

"Does that mean you're going to take pity on me?"

"Depends."

"On what?"

"First, is there food at your house? I always demand payment."

He blinked and looked around him, then looked at her again. They had all sat down for dinner. There had been huli huli chicken, kalua pork, ribs, rice, tons of salads and vegetables, and Liliha Bakery Cocoa Puffs. She had eaten a lot.

"Hey, are you with me, Seth?"

"You ate a lot."

"Way to romance a woman."

He smiled. "You do have the appetite of a Hobbit."

She rolled her eyes. "Have fun getting a ride home, loser."

As she turned to walk away from him, panic set in. He didn't know why, but something told him this was an important moment. Gently, he reached out for her arm. Soft, warm skin.

"Hey, sorry." He couldn't keep the laughter out of his voice. She was smiling when she turned to look over her shoulder at him.

"I need a piece of Mrs. Lui's haupia pie." The Hawaiian treat was similar to a French silk pie.

"Okay. Let me know when you're ready to leave."

She nodded, and he let her go.

"So, you don't need a ride home?" Ryan said from behind him. Dammit. He turned to face his team member standing a few feet behind him, with Maya beside him. "No. I'm fine."

"Nikki's feeling guilty."

And she should, but he shouldn't have reprimanded her the way he did.

"Gotcha. I'll take care of it."

He nodded. "We're headed out. Maya will get up at oh dark thirty."

"And you need a plate," Merri said as she hurried toward them, his mother beside her. "Do not leave me with all this food."

"I wouldn't think of it," Ryan said.

His mother gave him another kiss, and his parents left.

He glanced over at Nikki, who looked a bit miserable, and he decided to talk to her. It took him about fifteen minutes to make it over to her.

"Hey, Nikki. Sorry, I got onto you earlier. I shouldn't have."

She shook her head. "No, you were right. I know that I push it sometimes."

He studied her for a second or two. He saw the regret, but he also saw the self-loathing.

"You know you don't have to fit in with us."

She sighed as she studied the crowd. "That's easy for you to say."

"Have I made you feel you don't belong with us?"

She pulled her attention from the crowd to look at him. "No. In fact, you're the first commander I've ever had who has always made sure we felt like we belonged."

He knew she had been a squared-away Coastie. Still, he also understood that being in any of the services could be difficult for women. There were a lot of men who would never accept a woman's presence anywhere in the military except as a caregiver.

"Then...is there something someone else did?"

She sighed. "No. It's growing up in a family of men. I know that I overcompensate because of my size and my gender. I always have."

"You don't have to. You're our best team member."

Her eyes widened at his statement.

"You didn't really know?"

She shook her head. "I mean...even Kap?"

He nodded. "Don't get me wrong. In a fight, you're at a little bit of a disadvantage, mainly because of your stature. But I've seen you use that to your advantage. You did take Kap down just the other day. He's got a foot in height and probably around a hundred pounds on you. And he wasn't pulling any punches. That's why I make you grapple with him. Rami, he pulls his punches with you."

"What? He does not."

"He does. I think it's his upbringing. His mother is a bit of a terror, and while he respects you, it makes it hard to take you down."

She frowned. "I don't like that."

"Hey, he would follow you into a firefight. He respects you in the field. That's what's important."

He left unsaid that he was sure there was more behind Rami refusing to fight her at full strength, but that wasn't any of his business as long as it didn't interfere with work.

"But you fit in. Hell, I would say the team member closest to you in training and skills is probably Maya, but that's because she's a dog who can track by scent."

She laughed. "I thought maybe you were going to say something about both of us being bitches."

"I would never say that. But I'm guessing you had issues in the past with that?"

Her smile faded, and she nodded but didn't explain. "Again, I'm sorry about earlier."

"I was just being a little sensitive."

She shook her head. "No, I went over the line."

He knew there was something else she wanted to say. "Tell me."

"Y'all would make a cute couple."

He rolled his eyes. "I have a feeling Autumn wouldn't like that description."

Nikki laughed. "You should see the two of you together. She smiles a lot more around you."

"She's always cracking jokes."

"Yes, but she rarely smiles. Not real ones. When she's around you, she really smiles. And you do, too."

"I don't. I'm very stoic and manly."

She let out a belly laugh. "You are so fucking funny sometimes. Just, I would take a chance if I were you. You buzz when you're together. That's rare in our line of work. It's hard to trust someone and I have a feeling that you both trust each other."

"You trying to play matchmaker?"

She shrugged. "I just like seeing people happy. You two seem to understand each other."

"I don't understand her at all." The confession was out before he could control his tongue.

"Naw, you do. When Autumn was tweaking out the other day, you got her out of TFH and to a breakfast place."

"I went along with her."

"And let her talk. People always think she's so funny, but there's a loneliness beneath those sarcastic statements. I think you respond to it. You're good for each other."

"Oh, yeah, and what does she give me?"

"Someone to take care of. You're a caregiver, boss. Just think about it."

Then she left him, walking over to talk to Drew. He should

think this through and step back, but then he heard Autumn laugh. It wasn't that fake one she usually had, the one she used to distance herself from people. This was genuine. Sitting on the deck next to Maya, she talked to one of Del's kids. He found himself smiling as the two seemed to be in a deep discussion about something—probably a particular blue Australian dog because he knew they both loved the show.

Oh, damn. He wasn't falling for her. He *had* fallen headfirst for a woman he barely knew, who was keeping secrets from everyone.

ten

As Autumn pulled into Seth's driveway, she mentally started making excuses for not going into his house. Yes, she had insisted on him offering her food, but that was just a joke. She had things to do, like check back in with her hacker friend about a few things and check on Freddy.

"Don't even think about it."

She glanced at Seth. Even in the dim light from the street-light, he mesmerized her. There had always been something that drew her to him. He was gorgeous, even pretty for a man. Those eyelashes—they should be illegal. But there was something beneath the surface, something that was good and true.

And she was broken.

"Think about what, SEAL?"

His mouth twitched. "You want food, and I promised. Come on. Bring your container of food."

"I'm not sharing my leftovers with you."

He chuckled. "No, but you also don't want the bugs to get them."

True. Autumn slipped out of the car and followed him, carrying her container. Once in the house, he turned off his alarm as she slipped off her sandals. The wood floor was cool beneath her feet.

He led her down the hall to an open area with a nice-sized living area and a decent kitchen.

"Nice. Also, I'm trying to figure out how I ended up here."

It was true. It was like he was the pied piper or something. She would try to avoid him, and he just marched on, dragging her behind him.

"I'm used to commanding people," he said, taking her food container and putting it in his fridge. "I'll make sure you don't forget it."

A thousand butterflies exploded in her belly. This man.

"I don't need to be taken care of."

He crowded her against the kitchen counter, caging her in by putting a hand on either side of her hips.

"Yes, you do."

"I'm a grown woman who can handle herself."

He made a rude noise in the back of his throat. "Did I say you couldn't?"

"No."

"What I mean is, it's nice to have a soft place to land every now and then."

Her body went hot, her heart beating so hard against her chest she was sure there would be bruises. She had never been so charmed and turned on at the same time.

"You don't want to do this."

He leaned forward, his gaze connected to hers. He nipped at her bottom lip. "I think I know what I do and don't want."

"This is a mistake."

"We won't know until we make it. And let's be honest… mistakes are sometimes amazing."

She could hear the humor in his voice, the need that matched her own. Her nipples were hard, and it was taking every bit of her control not to lean forward and turn his butterfly kisses into something more.

"Mistakes can also cause a lot of problems."

"We've been dancing around this for months, Bradford. Why not see what happens when we both let go?"

"The consequences could be terrible."

"They could also be delicious."

She smiled, her defenses crumbling bit by bit. This man knew just what to say to get her to give in. And she wanted to. With every fiber of her being, she tried to fall into bed with this man. For just this night, she wanted to forget about everything and just feel.

She leaned forward and deepened their kiss, slipping her tongue into his mouth. Everything seemed to still, even the air around them, before he wrapped his arms around her waist and pulled her against him. She could feel his heart beating out of control precisely like hers. He tasted of temptation and something else—something she could never hope for. She regretted that…because this man would be wonderful to have in her life. She gave herself a quick second to regret that she wasn't a normal woman, then let it go. Soon, she wouldn't have a choice but to walk away to protect him, but she deserved this one night with him.

He lifted her up onto the counter, then kissed his way down her neck, nipping and licking her skin as he delved between her breasts. All the while, he was inching the skirt of her dress up her thighs, his callused fingers trailing along her skin. God, he was killing her with that mouth of his and the touch of his hands, and they were both fully dressed still.

He eased her back on the counter, then stilled as he pushed her dress up to reveal her bare pussy.

"Jesus," he muttered, his gaze zeroed in between her legs. "I would have never lasted if I had known you weren't wearing anything beneath this dress."

"I rarely wear underwear," Autumn said, her voice breathless, even to her own ears.

His gaze traveled up to capture hers. Darkened eyes, flushed skin. "I did not need to know that. You know that's all I'll think about whenever I'm around you?"

She blinked. "Sorry."

He took her hand and tugged her into a sitting position again, and she frowned. Was he so disgusted with her that he was done? She never understood these moments because she had only had fast, furious fucks, but now, he was looking at her with such tenderness and heat...it was odd. It made her stomach flutter.

"Don't *ever* apologize for being who you are, Autumn. You're an amazing woman who is as lethal with her sarcasm as she is with a gun. You. Are. Amazing."

She blinked once more, her chest warming, and, for some reason, she almost felt like crying. Sam and Ian always said things like that, but it was different coming from a man like Seth. They loved her like a relative. They *had* to say things like that.

"Thank you."

He stepped back, and she opened her mouth to argue with

him. She didn't get a chance. Instead, he yanked her off the counter into a standing position. Then, he bent and took hold of her, rising with her over his shoulder.

"What are you doing? And I'm too heavy for this."

He chuckled. "Darlin', I'm trained to carry men like this. You weigh practically nothing compared to that."

Oh, God. He had put a little twang in his accent. She knew he wasn't from the South, but damn, just that little bit had her wet. There was something so sexy about being called darlin' by a big, strong man. It went against everything she would typically want from a man, but it made her feel special.

He walked them down the hall and stepped into his bedroom. He tossed her on his bed. It surprised a laugh out of her as she bounced on the mattress. He had been advancing toward her when he paused.

"What?" she asked as he continued to stare at her.

"I love your laugh. Not the fake one you use with everyone else, but that one."

"How do you know I have a fake laugh?"

His mouth curled. Yep, she was a goner because she almost came from that little smile.

"I do. Maybe you don't realize it, but you hold back. Of course, I take credit for that laugh."

She loved it when he got cocky like that. "Oh, you do?"

He nodded as he took hold of the bottom of his shirt, tugged it over his head, and tossed it on the floor behind him. It was dark in the room, but, good God in heaven, the man was built. Muscle rippled beneath his flesh.

Every drop of moisture dried up in her mouth, and her fingers itched to explore all that.

"Yes."

"What?"

His mouth twitched. "Yes, I take credit for that laugh. But I also plan to take credit when you scream my name."

He joined her on the bed, crawling over her body until she was lying flat. He kissed her then while still balancing on his hands. Autumn wanted to feel his weight on her, have him crush her into the mattress.

The kiss was quick and wet, and she wanted more, but he pulled away.

"Nope. I've been dreaming about having my head between your legs for far too long."

Then Seth eased her dress up once again and settled between her legs. He kissed the top of her mound, his tongue barely teasing her clit before he pulled back.

Irritated, she tried to move closer, and a bark of laughter filled the room.

"Oh, no, you don't. I'm in charge of this."

"Excuse me?"

Another laugh. "Listen, you can tie me up and do whatever you want to me later. I don't care. But right now, I'm going to enjoy this delicacy, and all I want from you is your pleasure."

She was so stunned by the comment that she said nothing before he dipped his head again. This time, he licked her thigh leisurely, almost lovingly. Nope, she would not think that way. Men didn't think about her that way. She wasn't fragile or needed to be treated like something special.

He moved, but only to give her other thigh the same treatment. Finally, he worked his way up to her pussy. He pressed her legs apart further.

"Fuck, you're so wet."

That was definitely true. She was fairly dripping with need. He drew in a deep breath.

"Heaven."

It was all he muttered before he slid his hands beneath her ass to lift her up to his mouth. The moment his tongue slipped between her pussy lips, she was lost. Lost in pleasure, the feel of his mouth on her most intimate parts, and, dammit, she was lost in him. He was teasing her over and over, his tongue dipping into her just far enough to get her close to orgasm, then moving away before giving her completion.

Autumn wanted to demand that he finish her off and give her what she needed right now, but that would be a sign of weakness. She wasn't ready to share that with him now, not the soft underbelly of her heart. So, instead, she dug her fingers into the sheets as her toes curled.

He hummed against her before pulling back to slip his fingers up and inside of her. He curled them just right before adding his mouth once more. He took hold of her clit as he pumped his fingers in and out of her. At some point, she lost her mind, unable to really think at all. Instead, all she cared about was the pleasure he was promising her with his fingers and his mouth.

He lifted his mouth off her as he continued to thrust his fingers in and out of her. "Come for me, Autumn. Let go. I'll catch you."

Then he was on her again, this time driving her up and over that edge. Pleasure hit her hard, sending her over the edge into chaos. Every nerve ending in her body seemed to explode as delight washed over her entire body. She screamed his name, just as he had promised. He continued his onslaught as her orgasm faded, only to have another one explode in her so fast and hard it stole her breath.

He gave her pussy one last, long lick before he rolled out of bed. He had his pants off in record time. The man was a god. If his chest and shoulders took her breath away, the rest of him left her mute. He turned away to open his bedside table drawer, giving her a view of the most fantastic ass she had ever seen, like in person, not in a picture or on a video. She reached out and slipped her fingers over him. He smiled over his shoulder at her.

Oh, damn, that smile. It did weird things to her insides. It turned them mush, making her want things she couldn't have. She could only have this one night and needed to remind herself of that. It was all she could have, even if she didn't deserve it.

"You have a lot of clothes on, Bradford." His voice deepened and turned him even hotter. How did he keep getting hotter? Was it a SEAL thing?"

He turned to face her, his cock drawing her attention. Another beautiful part of this man. It was long, thick, with a drop of pearly pre cum wetting the head. She swung her legs off the side of the bed and sat up. Wrapping her fingers around his length, she pumped a couple of times before taking him into her mouth.

She tasted his precum, sweet and salty, then lost herself in exploring his cock, slipping her hand down to squeeze his balls. He groaned at that, causing her to look up at him. His gaze was blazing with heat.

"Look at you. You look so fucking pretty with my cock in your mouth."

He untied the knot of her halter dress so the fabric fell away. Cool air hit her breasts.

"I would like to squirt all over these, but first, I want to be inside of you when you come again."

She pulled back, releasing his cock. "Oh, you think you can make me come again?"

He laughed as he tugged her off the bed to her feet so they could get rid of her dress. It joined his clothes on the floor.

"Yeah, I know I can make you come again."

He quickly slipped on the condom, then tumbled them both back onto the bed. He landed on top of her, and she loved it. Usually, she didn't like a guy on top of her. It made her feel out of control. With Seth, it didn't seem to bother her. She was sure it meant something, but before she could figure it out, he took his cock in his hand, notching it against her center, before thrusting into her in one hard, deep move.

Their mingled groans filled the room. At that moment, it felt better than anything in her life. He held himself there for a moment. Then...he started to move. Slow and easy at first, bending down and taking a nipple into his mouth. The pleasure of being filled by him and the graze of his teeth against her sensitive tip was driving her insane. Slowly, surely, he teased her body, mind, and soul. This...this wasn't fucking. This was completely different, and she wasn't sure she was ready for that now.

Before she could order him to hurry up, he increased his rhythm. It was as if he could read her mind. He rose to his knees, dragging her hips up with him. It gave him the perfect angle, driving him impossibly deep inside of her. She could feel the orgasm right there, out of reach, and it was driving her crazy. Every nerve ending seemed on fire, ready to react to the release, but she couldn't do anything in this position. While she loved the feel of that cock of his slamming into her over and over as deep as he could go, she hated that she couldn't control anything.

"Let go, Autumn. I'll catch you."

He hit the perfect spot—or maybe it was the words. She exploded, screaming his name as pleasure washed over her, jolting down to her soul.

He followed her a moment later...his shout even louder as his fingers dug into her hips. He collapsed a little while later, right on top of her. She grunted.

"Dude, you weigh a ton."

He chuckled as he rose up, resting his weight on his elbows on the mattress. He stared down at her long enough for the back of her throat to tickle. She opened her mouth to say something, anything, to make light of the situation.

"Don't."

"What?"

"Don't make a joke. Let me enjoy this moment."

She wanted to argue with him, but something had her holding her thoughts in.

"And don't do that. You don't have to hide from me. Just don't pretend this didn't mean anything. We might not know what it is, but it is something,"

She didn't like that idea. It made her itchy from the inside out, thinking it could be more. And sad. So unbearably sad.

He reached up and pushed her hair back from her face. "Stay right here."

He slipped out of her, then out of bed, getting rid of the condom before coming back to bed.

"I might have had plans," she said as he pulled her into his arms.

"If it's screaming my name a few more times, then I'm down with that. Let's get some rest first."

She couldn't help but smile as she snuggled closer. "You think a lot of yourself."

"Yeah, I do. Go to sleep, Bradford."

"Shut up, SEAL."

Then, she quickly drifted off, knowing it was a mistake to stay, but she couldn't force herself to leave. Just this once, she would indulge.

eleven

THE SCENT of cinnamon pulled Seth out of a deep sleep. Before his eyes were open, he reached for Autumn but found the bed empty. Weak sunlight peeked from behind the blinds. He hadn't slept in like this for...well, months. He had been on edge since he separated from the Navy. Heading up Team Bravo hadn't been easy, even if it was something he loved. The TFH *'ohana* had made it easy. Seth hadn't realized how stressed he had been since settling in Honolulu.

Of course, he knew the biggest stressor had been the woman who had spent the night in his bed. And she had left him alone...but that didn't explain the smell of cinnamon.

Sitting up, he glanced around the room, noting that her dress was on the chair in the corner, so she hadn't left. All of a sudden, he felt lighter and happier.

Yes, he was rested, and it made sense. The mind-blowing sex had a lot to do with it, but still, they had been up a lot throughout the night. He was sure he hadn't gotten as much sleep as usual. He felt fantastic. He wondered where Autumn was and why his house suddenly smelled like Christmas.

He slipped out of bed, went to the bathroom, brushed his teeth, and pulled on sweatpants. Padding barefoot and topless, he went in search of Autumn. It was easy to see her when he stepped into the living room. She was at his stove, cooking something. And she was wearing one of his shirts.

He swallowed as something shifted inside of him. He had never been a man who believed in falling so fast.

Lust? Yeah. Been there, done that. A lot.

But this...was different. Seth wanted this morning for the rest of his life. It had nothing to do with what she was doing, but it was her being here, her hair a mess of curls, wearing his shirt.

His shirt.

"Are you going to keep standing there like a goober staring, or are you going to come in here and help?" she asked, her voice full of humor. She didn't even turn around to look at him, and he was a goner.

"I was trying to figure out what you were doing."

Autumn grinned at him over her shoulder. His world shifted. "That explains why I had to order things to cook this morning. Like, how do you survive on protein bars? Gross."

Then she turned around as if it was just ordinary for her to stand there in his shirt and cook him breakfast.

He approached her, unsure what to do with all the feelings bombarding him. Panic rode alongside the need, now twisting in his gut.

"So, you *do* cook."

She slanted him a sly look. "Of course I do. I'm especially good at French toast, which I hope you like because I would hate to sit in front of you and eat it all. Made coffee." She nodded to his coffee pot.

He poured himself a mug as he watched her. The thick bread sizzled in butter in his very seldom-used skillet.

"I just assumed you couldn't cook."

"I told you I could cook. Did you not believe me?"

"Sometimes you say things just to fuck with people."

There was a beat of silence, and then she threw her head back and laughed. The sound filled the kitchen with even more warmth.

"You do know me well. Also, if you tell anyone, I'll call you a lying bastard."

She grabbed one of the plates she had set out, piled a few slices, and handed it to him. Then she made a plate for herself. He waited for her to sit at the bar, then sat beside her.

Autumn didn't wait for him to eat. She dug into her food with wild abandon—after drowning it in syrup, of course.

When she realized he was just watching her, she looked at him. "What?"

"I like watching you eat."

She rolled her eyes. "I have to sustain a high metabolism, and after last night's activities, I'm worn out. I knew you would be good, but you have the stamina of a sex god."

He felt his cheeks flush, and she giggled.

"Oh. My. Gawd. Did I just embarrass you?"

Seth chuckled. "You're plain speaking."

"I thought guys liked that." Now she was frowning, her eyes looking worried. She looked so damned vulnerable, something he wasn't used to seeing. He thought back to everything she'd told him. She had been raised in a bubble, without regular interactions outside of the cult. He was sure she sometimes had difficulty understanding all people, not just men.

"I do. It's just that I've never been compared to a god before."

"A sex god. Not just an ordinary god."

He shook his head and started eating before his food got cold. The moment the custardy confection hit his taste buds, he moaned. He wasn't a foodie, but damn.

"I'm good. Say it."

He swallowed his bite. "Damn, why don't you want people to know you can cook like this?"

Autumn sighed. "It goes back to my upbringing. Joseph didn't think women could be good at anything other than the household things. Cooking, cleaning, having babies…he said we were too stupid."

"What an asshole."

"Exactly."

"So you decided to go into law enforcement. Was that to spite him?"

"It was to find him."

He blinked. "You've always thought he was alive? I thought they found DNA at the compound."

She shrugged. "I know it makes me sound like a nut, but they said he was there taking care of the people. That was never a thing he did. He would let other people do all the work, even die if need be. He would not go down with the ship. So, after talking about it with Sam and Ian, I decided to go into law enforcement. Sam wanted me to enter MI-6, but I didn't want to do spy work. Too dirty for my tastes."

He frowned.

"Don't worry. I know I sound like a nut, but with what happened with Jin and the Alana Kim case, I feel he's still out there." She shrugged. "He was always into drugs, especially synthetics."

"You're telling me he was a drug dealer."

"Yeah, well, among other things. Joseph was a cheap conman in the truest sense. He scammed people out of their life savings, whether it was preaching to them or selling them drugs. We've—"

"We?"

"Sam, Ian, and I. We went through his history. Joseph wasn't even his real name. Donald Reynolds. That was his real name. He did just about everything he could to make people earn money for him."

"Just drugs?"

"Nope. He was a pimp too. Great guy, my mother picked to shack up with, huh?"

He wanted to dig deep into her thoughts and not just because of work. He wanted to know more about her, and whether she liked the fact or not, Joseph was a big part of her life. But he could feel her retreating back into the Autumn she showed other people, and he didn't want that. He wanted the teasing woman who made him one of the best French toasts he had ever had.

"What are your plans this weekend? Are you doing anything with Sam?"

She shook her head. "It takes him a bit to acclimate to time change, so he'll relax. I took a couple days off next week to hang out with him."

Which was a good thing since she was a workaholic, but now he was jealous of the man who was a surrogate father.

"How about we spend some time in bed ourselves?"

She blinked, then her mouth curled into a smile. He did

that. He made her smile. For some reason, he felt as if he owned the whole damned world.

"Are you proposing we have sex all day?"

"In between napping. We aren't on call this weekend, and I know we could get called out at any time, but we have our cells."

"I expect lunch and dinner."

"Of course," he said before shoving the last bite of his French toast into his mouth.

"Then you have a deal."

Her voice was lighter, and he wanted to do that more. He needed to make her feel like it was okay to tell him things, and, in the end, it didn't change how he felt about her. Although he didn't want to put a name on it, he had a feeling this wasn't just a weekend fling.

"I'll clean up," he said, taking her plate and rising to his feet.

"I cook, so you clean?"

"Yes. You sit there and drink your coffee."

"And admire your amazing body and the fact that you decided to wear grey sweatpants?"

"What is up with that? Women online are always going on about them. He rinsed off the plates and put them in the dishwasher, along with the silverware and bowls she'd used for prep.

"There is just something about the way they look on a man. I mean, they don't hide anything."

He felt his cheeks heat again, which was disconcerting. How was this woman making him blush? He was a former SEAL, for God's sake.

"You're blushing again, aren't you?"

He shook his head and finished up. When he turned around, he found her smiling at him over her coffee cup. The sunlight filled the kitchen and brought out the red highlights in her hair. She was wearing one of his white shirts, and he wanted this just like when he first saw her this morning. He wanted her smiling at him like that every day for the rest of his life.

He waited for the panic to rise. But it never arrived. Instead, he realized that nothing had ever felt this right in his life. It should worry him. No woman had gotten under his skin this fast.

But he pushed that aside. He wanted to make sure he didn't freak her out. So, instead, he smiled.

"Now, let's talk payment."

One eyebrow rose.

"*That* was payment. For your breakfast."

"Tsk, tsk, Ms. Bradford. You didn't negotiate that. I said I would do it, not why I was doing it."

She must have read the intent in his gaze because she let out a squeal of delight before she took off running. Seth knew she could run faster than she was, so she was letting him catch up to her. He scooped her up in his arms and carried her bridal style into his bedroom, then into his bathroom.

"What do you have in mind, SEAL?"

Her voice was breathless as he dropped her on the vanity. It was a double vanity with a space between the two sinks, giving him all kinds of ideas. Cupping her face, he leaned in, brushing his mouth over hers. She kissed him quickly, willingly, making those little mewling noises that sent heat soaring within him. His cock was hard and dripping, and that told him he should get them both in the shower.

He turned the water on, then tugged her off the counter and into the stand-up shower. One of the reasons he wanted to rent this house had been this shower. It was large with one of those raindrop shower heads. After shutting the door, he positioned her so that she sat on the bench.

"Getting kind of pushy, SEAL."

God, he loved her voice when she was happy. It was one of the best sounds in the world, but he knew the sounds he liked better.

He dropped down and leaned forward to kiss her stomach. He saw a small scar.

"What's this?"

"What's what?"

He traced the incision scar with his tongue. "That."

She didn't hesitate. "Knife wound. Bad op."

He wanted to ask her more, but not right now. Right now, all that mattered was making her come. He placed a hand on each of her thighs, moved her legs apart, and decided it was time for another treat. Licking her slit from the bottom all the way up to her clit, he hummed. God, she was delicious. It was as if she were every dream he had ever had and a few more he didn't know he had. As he slipped his tongue between her pussy lips, she moaned.

Fuck. He couldn't remember ever having a woman respond to him this way. As she slipped her fingers through his wet hair, he pressed a finger inside of her as he teased her clit with his teeth. It only took him a minute or two before he had her screaming his name. Her voice echoed off the tiled walls.

He pulled her up off the bench and reversed their positions. Then he realized he'd forgotten a condom. Before he could say anything, she climbed on his lap.

"Wait."

She looked down at him. Her hair was a mass of wet curls.

Water dripped from her nipples. He was surprised he didn't come right then.

"Condom."

"Are you clean?"

He nodded.

"I am too, and I take a shot."

"Thank God," he said as she took his cock in hand and positioned herself over it. She sank down on him, her inner muscles clinging hard around his shaft.

He took a nipple in his mouth as she continued to ride him, hard and faster, until he felt his orgasm approaching. He reached down between the two of them to tease her clit, once more sending her over the edge. She came a second before he did. He thrust up into her and held her tight against him, his orgasm seemingly endless.

They were both breathing heavily as she collapsed on top of him. After a few moments, he turned off the water, lifted her off him, and dried them both off before they stumbled back to bed.

She snuggled up against him, her head on his chest above his heart, as they drifted off to sleep.

twelve

"I DON'T UNDERSTAND why you have to leave?" Seth said, acting like a pouty little boy. It was actually kind of cute.

"Because I need clothes," Autumn said for about the third time. She had said she would stay all day, but that was before she got the text about an early meeting tomorrow. Yes, she needed clothes, but she also needed space. It was fun to play with a man like Seth, but she also knew it would end one way or another. She just hoped he didn't hate her either way.

"You look great in my clothes."

"Thank you, but I need underwear."

"You don't wear underwear."

She chuckled. He was sitting on his bed, trying to entice her back in for another bout of lovemaking. Stepping in between his legs, she took his face in her hands.

"We have work tomorrow. I need to get home and go over some case files. I have a meeting with the DA about that Ortiz case. I even think the FBI will be there."

"Stop being responsible. It makes you irresistible."

She was smiling when she leaned down to press her mouth against his. She expected it to be a slow kiss, but it soon got out of hand. She was tempted to stay but knew she had things to do.

Her phone buzzed in her pocket. With a lot of regret, she pulled back.

"Let me guess, Ian."

She pulled her phone out.

> Ian: Where the bloody hell are you?

> Autumn: I was resting after a lot of sex.

> Ian: *throwing up in mouth gif*

She smiled and slipped her phone back into her pocket.

"Yep, but now he won't bother me for a while."

"Did you threaten him?"

"No. I told him I'd had a lot of sex. He'll leave me alone for a few hours now."

He chuckled. "You two definitely act like siblings."

She wanted to tell him everything in that instant. This was a first for her. Sam and Ian were the only ones who knew her entire story. No matter how close she got to other people, she never could trust them with her deep, dark secrets. Seth was different. She wanted to tell him everything, but she couldn't. It would endanger him, and she couldn't allow that.

"What? Where did you just go?"

"Sorry, my mind just slipped back into work mode."

Not really a lie because she had always seen her career as a means to an end.

"Okay."

She could tell from his tone that he didn't believe her, but he would let it go. She knew it was only a matter of time before he started to ask more questions.

"So, how do we play this tomorrow?"

She frowned. "What do you mean?"

"At work."

She sighed. "Can we keep it between us for now?"

He cocked his head as he studied her. "For now?"

She nodded. If she survived whatever was brewing with Joseph, she wouldn't mind having something more with Seth— if he forgave her for lying to him.

"I want to ensure we know what we want before everyone starts weighing in. TFH is ʻohana, and they tend to be nosey—if you haven't noticed."

He chuckled as he rose from the bed, taking her hand. "Yeah, they are."

He walked her out to her car. She was glad she always carried a go bag in her car, so she didn't have to do a walk of shame.

"I guess I'll see you tomorrow," he said, still pouting.

She leaned up and gave him a quick, hot, wet kiss, then she slipped into her car. She backed out of the drive and drove down his street. When she looked up in her mirror, she noticed he was still watching her, his hands in the pockets of those damned grey sweatpants.

Those damned butterflies were back. He made her feel safe. Sam and Ian did for the most part, but they had to since they were family. Seth saw her as something more than an obligation. And that made her feel almost giddy.

It was Sunday afternoon, so it didn't take her long to get into Honolulu. When she pulled into the parking lot of her building, she was stopped by HPD, who had taped off the area. Her whole body went on alert. After parking her car, she approached one of the young officers.

"What happened?" she asked after showing the officer her badge.

"Druggie overdosed. Nothing that big."

Her entire soul turned to ice. "Druggie?"

He nodded. "A guy named Freddy."

A weird buzzing sounded in her head as if she were about to pass out. She knew it wasn't a simple overdose. She had no proof, but she knew Joseph had something to do with this. Her phone buzzed, and she rolled her eyes, thinking it was Ian, but everything around her faded away when she saw the screen.

> Unknown: I see you found out about Freddy.

He could see her. She knew he could, and that's why she had been conscientious about people seeing her in public and why she had this stupid, gross apartment. But this was the first time he'd contacted her since she stole away that night all those years ago.

> Autumn: What up, loser?

She knew that would anger him.

> Unknown: You would think you would be more careful with your mocking, considering who I have here with me.

Then a picture came through of Sam, but it wasn't really Sam. This Sam had a clean-shaven face and weighed about thirty pounds heavier than he was now. Sam had a beard now, so whatever they based it on was an old pic. But she didn't want Joseph to know. If he thought she would be erratic that would be best.

> Autumn: What do you want?

He sent her a pin on the map on the island's other side. Was he really that stupid? Would he just give up his position? She looked up and over the rooftops. She knew precisely what camera he was using and where. She stared at it for a long moment, then drew her thumb across her neck. She turned and headed back to her car without responding to his text. There was a chance that he could read her texts if he had gotten into the CCTV around the area.

She was ready for this to be over. And hopefully, Ian, Sam, and Seth would forgive her for not calling on them. They would just have to understand she was doing this to protect them.

"Do you think that's the smart move, sir?" Peter asked him.

The man known as Joseph Watters studied the idiot. He knew the younger man meant well, but other things were at play. In the end, Joseph didn't care what happened to Peter. He was a minion, a man Joseph used to do his dirty work. Once he had what was rightfully his, he couldn't care less what happened to the man.

"Yes."

"She has to know that is a fake picture."

"Does that matter? It's your fault that we don't have that druggie to use as bait."

Once again, he was surrounded by idiots. He wanted his old friend Hank back, but he had been dumb enough to get arrested and think he could turn Joseph over to the police. Having Hank killed had been sad, but it had to be done.

"I'm sorry, sir. I tried, but he fought me."

He had wanted to draw the game out a little longer, maybe get her on board, but he heard the promo for the *Beyond Murder* podcast. Summer Joy was spilling his secrets. People would start looking for him. Yes, maybe he had panicked and ordered Patrick to bring him Freddy. Who would have thought that stupid bastard would fight with Patrick.

Joseph had watched everything go down, but he refused to admit it. Instead, he wandered away, looking out the window. A *True Believer* had allowed him to stay at the house free of charge. It was in the middle of nowhere, and you had to have money to have a house like that on Oahu. Joseph had blown through much of the money he'd earned in his last venture in Malaysia. Now, he had no choice but to get his daughter's money.

"Sir, are you sure this was a good idea?"

It was the second time in the space of a minute that this asshole thought he had the right to question Joseph. During his tenure as the leader of Joyous Wave, no one had questioned his authority. He had been in charge, and they had been his minions.

"She has no idea, and she wasn't about to text or call him."

"That's what I find odd. Autumn—"

He spun on his heel and took two large steps to grab hold of the boy. And that was what he was. Only in his mid-twenties with dark brown hair and brown, dull eyes...he was expendable. Joseph grabbed him by the collar of his shirt and yanked him forward.

"Her name is Summer Joy. Don't call her by that made-up name."

He held the boy until he nodded, then tossed him. Peter stumbled back against the wall, gasping for breath. He lowered his eyes. Fuck, Joseph wished he still had his members from long ago. The remaining idiots weren't as well disciplined as the genuine cult members. These *True Believers* were wannabes. They didn't understand how to deal with people like his daughter.

"We need my money to thrive. This newest drug is being pulled off the street left and right."

Peter said nothing. Instead, he kept his eyes down and just nodded.

Good. The Summer arrived, the faster he would be rid of all these idiots.

It had only been a couple of hours, and Seth was at odds. He'd texted his mother, who said they thought they might be ready for lunch tomorrow. He understood it. The stress of moving and all of that was a lot. Besides, he didn't want to spend time with anyone other than Autumn.

That was a little worrying. Due to his job in the Navy, Seth had only had a couple longer relationships. They didn't last that long, but he also didn't obsess about them like he had about Autumn.

He knew she could take care of herself, but something in him wanted to take care of her, too. He had a feeling she rarely let people know her that well. Yes, she supported the team members, but if you asked one of them if they'd ever helped her out, they wouldn't be able to come up with anything. He was sure of it.

As Nikki had said, he had always been a protector. And the one person he wanted to protect was Autumn.

His doorbell alert went off before banging ensued on his front door.

"Open up," a cultured British voice shouted out.

Seth frowned as he opened the door to reveal Ian.

"Where the hell is Autumn?"

"What do you mean?"

He pushed past Seth and stalked through his house.

"Come on in, Ian. Nice to have you."

The former spy ignored him. "Autumn!"

His irritation faded when he heard the panic in Ian's voice. Ice slid down his spine as he took in the other man's appearance. His hair looked like he hadn't combed it in days, his shirt was a wrinkled mess, and he wore jeans. Seth had never seen the man in anything other than dress pants. Ian even had a day's worth of whiskers on his face. There was something really wrong.

"What's going on? Why don't you just text her?"

He stopped in front of Seth. "I did. That's why I want to know what you did with her."

"I said goodbye to her after lunch. She said she had things to do. Something about a meeting with the DA this week about the Ortiz trial."

But as soon as he said it, icy fingers slid down his spine,

leaving his blood cold and his entire body alert. "Fuck. She never texted me when she got home."

He grabbed his phone and texted her.

> Seth: Your brother is here, and he is freaking out.

Nothing. In fact, he was pretty sure her phone was off because it wasn't delivered.

"Nothing?" Ian asked, his face actually looked hopeful.

Seth shook his head. "When was the last time you had contact with her?"

"This morning, when she sent me that horrible text, then she disappeared. Fucking hell." He texted someone on his phone. "Letting Dad know. He's worried."

Seth nodded as he called Adam.

"Please tell me you have a good reason to call me the day after my engagement party." Amusement laced his words, and Seth almost regretted doing this, but he had no choice.

"Have you heard from Autumn?"

"No, not since she left with you. Did you have problems closing the deal? I'll give you some pointers."

There was a murmur in the background, and he was sure it was Jin.

"It's Seth. He's looking for Autumn."

There was a jostling of the phone, and then Jin came on the line.

"Seth. When was the last time you heard from her?"

"After lunch. She said she had to prep the Ortiz case."

"I'm going to get hold of Sam."

"We already talked to him."

She paused, then sighed. "No. Not her father. Her friend

Sam. She might be able to find out where she is or at least have an idea. I'll tell Adam if we find anything."

"Thank you."

"No problem."

Then she was gone, and Adam was back on the line. "So, you talked to her father? What about Ian?"

He clicked on the speaker. "He's here with me, and I just put you on speaker."

"Good. So, the last time you saw her was today?"

"Yeah. And Ian hasn't heard from her."

"Your father, Ian?"

"No. We've been texting her for over an hour. She hasn't read the messages."

"That means we might have a missing team member. All hands on deck, Seth. Call everyone in and ensure Maya and Ryan are on board because we might need your team to go out. I'll call Del and my team in."

"Gotcha."

He hung up and sent a group text to the team.

> Seth: We have a situation. I need everyone at headquarters ASAP. This is not an exercise. We have a missing TFH team member.

> Kap: Roger that.

> Ryan: On our way.

> Nikki: I'm on the North Shore. Will get there ASAP.

> Rami: Gotcha.

He looked at Ian. "I take it you want to come in with me?"

Ian nodded.

"Give me a second, and I'll be ready to leave."

As he rushed about getting changed and putting on his gear, he sent up a silent prayer. He wished he could say this was just a misunderstanding, but because no one could seem to get hold of Autumn, something had happened, and he was going to move heaven and earth to get to her.

thirteen

SETH STRODE off the elevator into the common area, which normally would be dead on a Sunday afternoon. Instead, it was buzzing with activity. Del had his wife with them as they looked over something on a tablet. His team stood on the opposite side of the room discussing different rescue scenarios, and Adam had his team in another area. They all seemed to be on the phone, probably checking in with other people.

"Wow," Ian said under his breath.

"One of us goes missing, the entire group will be here to help." He glanced at Ian. "You doubted that?"

"No." He shrugged. "A lot of people think she's flighty."

Seth snorted as he dropped his gear in his office. "Autumn isn't flighty. She's solid as an investigator with excellent instincts. She also knew this would happen if she didn't answer the texts and phone calls. Autumn would never let all these people worry about her for no reason."

He stepped further into his office and motioned with his head. Ian followed him. Seth shut the door, knowing this had to be discussed, even though Autumn was going to be pissed that he'd figured it out. On the way in, he would have questioned Ian, but he had chosen to drive his car instead of riding in with Seth.

"I want to talk to you about your relationship with Autumn."

Ian rolled his eyes. "Is there time for this?"

"Yes, because it factors into the investigation."

"Don't worry, mate, I won't step on your toes. She's not my kind of woman."

This family. They made his head hurt.

"Stop the bullshit. I'm not worried about you."

Ian's smug smile dissolved as he studied Seth's face. "She told you?"

"Nope. I just started putting it together with a few other things. So, why don't you tell me."

"Her mother and my father had a love affair when he was in the States."

"And?"

"Yeah, Autumn was the result. What made you realize it?"

He thought back to this morning when he was kissing down her body in the shower. The small scar on her abdomen had grabbed his attention.

"What's this?"

"Knifed during an op."

"Your father had a transplant last year, right?"

Ian nodded.

"She has a scar on her abdomen. When I asked about it, she lied."

"Yeah, she was the best candidate and, like always, she didn't hesitate, although she had to reveal her connection to Dad to Adam and Del."

"Does Joseph know?"

Another long pause. "You believe her? That Joseph is still alive?"

"You do, too."

He nodded. "Yeah, we've been tracking him for a decade. All three of us."

"Joseph still thinks she's his daughter?"

"We think so. We don't think he would be here otherwise."

Seth opened his mouth to ask what he meant by that when there was a sharp knock on his door before it slammed open.

"Harry, we need you out here," Tamilya said. "Charity found something."

They followed Tamilya out into the common area. Their forensic tech, Charity, had a tablet in her hand. Her FBI husband was off to the side on the phone. He was probably checking in with contacts as the liaison between the two organizations.

"I started looking for Autumn, wondering what could have happened to her. I tracked her phone to this apartment building in Honolulu."

Seth looked at the area and shook his head internally. They would talk about her living situation as soon as they could.

He noticed there was an area taped off by the HPD.

"Damn, that Freddy had to go and overdose," Ian said.

"Someone you know?"

"Autumn used him as an informant sometimes."

Seth noticed Del texting someone. "I'll have Elle check out the info on the body. It probably went to HPD for their analysis, but she has a good relationship with the crew there."

"What is she doing?" Ian muttered, drawing Seth's attention back to the screen. He watched as she pulled out her phone and started texting with someone. Then, she looked around as if searching for someone. He saw the moment she zeroed in on the CCTV. She looked at the camera, then drew her thumb across her neck.

His head spun as his blood froze. She was threatening someone, and knowing her, she planned to go after whoever she'd been texting.

Joseph. She was going after that crazy bastard and had been missing for at least two hours.

"What the hell is going on here?"

Everyone turned to find Sam watching them.

"We're looking for Autumn," Ian said, irritation filtering through his voice. Seth got it. He was worried about his sister and didn't want to deal with their father, too. But he also knew that any paternal instinct would have this man ready to fight.

"Do you have anything yet?"

Ian shook his head. "Just an interaction over the phone."

He looked at Charity. "Could you play it back?"

"Of course."

They all watched in silence once more.

"Can you track her?" he asked, reminding Seth again that he had been a spy, a type of law enforcement. The man understood precisely what could happen to her.

Charity shook her head. "But I have her last location when the phone was on."

A map appeared on the screen. Oh, damn, Autumn was in the middle of nowhere, but the pinpoint gave them at least a starting point. He would find her if it was the last thing he did. His team was already gearing up and preparing for the rescue.

"Wait," Del said. "You need to know what you're walking into. You don't even know what this is about."

"I do. It's about Joseph Watters still being alive."

Everyone seemed to stop moving at the same time.

"The cult leader who died in the fire?" TJ, Charity's FBI spouse, asked.

He nodded.

"There was DNA," TJ said.

"Watters had a lot of connections in state government and law enforcement at the time," Adam said. "Jin has been researching him since she investigated the Alana Kim murder a few months ago. I have to agree with Seth on this. Jin is sure the man is alive and had someone fake his dental and DNA records. He could have done it."

"Why is he after Autumn then?" TJ asked. It was a fair question, but he didn't care. All he wanted to do was get the fuck out of there to find her.

"Money." This came from Emma, Del's wife. They all turned to face her.

"Say again?" Del asked.

"Money. That's all Joseph has ever cared about. He wants her money."

"What kind of money? She's a civil servant," Del said.

Emma sighed, then looked at Ian. "Are you going to say anything?"

Seth looked at her brother, then to Sam. "Okay, spill right now. We need to know everything."

Ian made a face, but Sam stepped up. "You've heard of Bradford Industries?"

"It went defunct a while ago," Charity said. "The family died out."

At that moment, everyone put the pieces together. Seth sighed. "They didn't go defunct?"

Sam shook his head. "No. They sold off their business, and the money went into a trust for Autumn. She came into the money just over a year ago."

He thought back to the apartment building she lived in, the way she acted...

"How much?"

"She'd be a billionaire if she hadn't given a lot of it away."

He rolled his shoulders, trying to push away the discomfort. Autumn didn't owe him all her secrets, and they were new to each other. She didn't know everything about him, but then, he wasn't a millionaire.

"And Joseph plans on getting her money? How? And isn't this just a little elaborate to get the money?"

"That bastard always liked games," Sam muttered. "Plus, Autumn is convinced he blames her for his downfall."

Revenge and greed. Watters wanted to make her pay, first with her money, then with her life. There was no way Seth was going to let that happen.

He nodded. "We're heading out. Keep us updated on the location if it changes, Charity."

Ian stopped him by grabbing him by the elbow. "I'm coming."

Ian was dressed down from his usual suit slacks and button-down shirts, but he wasn't dressed for a rescue.

"Listen, I get it. She's important to you." He looked at Sam. He didn't think many people knew about their blood connection, and it wasn't his place to reveal it. "To both of you. This is what I do for a living. We work as a team and know each other in the field. You would be a hindrance. Also, you can get some gear here if something else comes up. This is our first lead, but something else might pop up."

Ian sighed, then nodded.

"Plus, I think you might have some connections, so we can get some satellite imagery to help?"

"Yes. I'll call a few people," Sam said. The smiling man from the night before had turned into a hardened warrior. Seth would not want to be Joseph Watters at the moment.

He walked away, already on the phone with someone.

Seth looked at Ian.

"Bring her home."

"If it's the last thing I do, I will get her back." Seth made sure the other man understood his feelings for Autumn. It was new and raw, but he loved her. He didn't know how he fell so fast and hard for a woman who hid so much from him, but he did. Seth knew she wouldn't be happy about it, but they would deal with that once he got her back.

Ian studied him for a second, then his eyes widened. He nodded and stepped back. Just as Seth stepped toward the front doors, Del's phone pinged. Seth wanted to growl but buried that feeling and turned to see what other news had come in.

"Okay, Elle got the report. It wasn't an overdose. Blunt force trauma to the back of the head. He was murdered."

"Autumn will be out for blood. She had a soft spot for him. If Joseph killed him to get to Autumn..." Ian sighed. "She's going to be more erratic."

Seth nodded. Autumn was like him, a protector. This time, though, she would learn that it was time to let someone else protect her.

Autumn drew in a deep breath, her body aching from the run through the jungle and the guard she took down. Fucking Joseph couldn't just do something as simple as confronting her. No, he had her traipsing through a jungle filled with bugs and assholes he'd hired.

Maybe she should have waited, or maybe she should have driven up to the house. And yes, she should have contacted the team somehow. She wasn't usually erratic like this. One thing Sam had taught her was to always have a plan.

About half-way to her destination, she had realized her mistake. Going in without backup was stupid. Still, she knew that there was a good chance Joseph was following her progress through the traffic cams. Just how long had he been watching her? That's why she always felt eyes on her, at least these last few weeks. Either way, her impulsive behavior might have been a mistake, but she'd made sure to leave lots of clues for the team.

There was also a chance that something really bad had happened to Sam and that's why they had the really bad fake picture. Joseph had always been a loser surrounded by losers, but that didn't mean he couldn't have tried to get to Sam.

Just as she had that thought, she heard a twig snap behind her. She turned to confront the guard, then had to look up. *Great.* He was massive. He was close to six-foot-five and probably outweighed her by at least one hundred and fifty pounds, with a large scar down his right cheek. He was bald with Pacific Islander features.

"Mr. Watters wants to talk to you."

She knew he did and should let this behemoth take her in. It would be easier and faster, but it was also what Joseph wanted. And one thing she had learned was that giving Joseph what he wanted wasn't worth the price. She knew she would get taken in. Hell, she was heading to his house, but the asshole wanted her humiliated.

"I don't give a fuck."

His eyes widened. "You need to come with me."

"So, is Sam at the house?"

He didn't say anything, but he looked away briefly. That told Autumn that she had been right. Thank God.

"You need to come with me," he said again.

She settled her weight, getting ready for a fight. "Make me."

There was a long beat of silence. The dripping of water and the bugs buzzing were the only sounds between them. Slowly, his mouth curved, then turned into a grin that sent ice coursing through her blood. He was missing two front teeth. Lovely. He was definitely a *True Believer*.

He launched at her, trying to take her down, but she quickly thwarted him. He was big, but that size made it hard for him to move. She slipped beneath his arm as he reached for her, hurrying to get behind him. Her triumph was short-lived when he twisted around and grabbed her arm. Fuck, his fingers dug into her flesh as she tried to yank it free.

"It would be easier if you would just come in. You're here to see him."

That was true, and it was stupid to fight this, but she wanted to go in on her terms. If she was going to possibly die, she would do it the way *she* wanted to. That meant mainly being a pain in the ass. Also, the more time she spent fighting them, the more time TFH would have.

She relaxed her arm. The guy did have an advantage because of his size, but she had a good idea that he wasn't that smart.

"Fine. But can you let go of my arm? I think you've bruised me. Not sure Joseph will like that."

His eyes widened, fear stamped on his features. These *True Believers* always thought Joseph had special abilities. He loosened his hold, and she yanked her arm out and turned to run.

"Summer Joy!"

Yep. They all called her by her former name. She ran through the jungle area, sure she was stomping through filming scenes for the show about the people stranded on an island. There was also a good chance she could run into a wild boar, and those things scared her more than the giant now traipsing after her. Jesus, she thought she was loud.

But as she thought she had just gotten away over a ridge, a massive body ran into her from the right, taking her down. It wasn't the other guard, but someone just as enormous. They hit the ground so hard that Autumn knew he'd knocked the air out of her. Her head hit something hard, and pain vibrated from her temple, exploding through her body.

The first guard stopped just a few steps away from her.

"Tsk, tsk, Summer Joy. We could have done this the easy way. Look what you made Bart do."

"Bart?"

She turned to look at the idiot approaching her. "Your name is Bart?"

He opened his mouth to say something but didn't get the chance. Instead, her head started to spin.

Her last thought was that she hoped TFH followed the clues she left, and then her entire world turned black.

fourteen

AS THEY MADE their way through the forest, Seth pushed back on his panic. He didn't know Joseph, but what he did know wasn't good. Since he had been declared dead for over a decade, who knew what kind of mental state he was in. If he planned on stealing Autumn's money, then he definitely did have a screw loose. He would have to come forward as her father to get it.

Those thoughts kept swirling in his head, even as he kept moving one foot in front of the other.

He heard Maya bark, and he turned. That was the sound he had been praying for. They followed the dog to an area where the vegetation had been disturbed. Yep, there had been a fight there, at least three individuals. Two larger people—definitely men—then smaller tracks.

Autumn.

His heart leaped up and almost choked him. She had left her car in an area where it would be easily found, then —if he was reading the signs correctly—she had left them all kinds of clues to her trail.

"Here, Captain," Kap said, pointing to a rock. "There's some blood."

Even as every drop of his blood chilled, he nodded. He could not lose his mind because she was counting on them. Thankfully, it didn't look like a lot of blood, but at least it was a sign.

Maya barked and strained against her lead.

"Let's go," he ordered as they started off in the direction Maya was telling them to go.

Hold on, Autumn. We're coming.

Autumn woke slowly to darkness. For a few moments, her brain didn't want to work. It was almost like her head had a puzzle with a few pieces missing. Speaking of her head, it was pounding like a freaking hammer. Gingerly, she sat up and sucked in a breath. Fuck, her ribs hurt.

Then...the events came rushing back to her. Freddy being killed, Joseph texting her, and the fight in the woods with Bart and his friend. Then...nothing.

She had left her phone back in the car, knowing that the area she was in had little to no cell service. Instead, she waited until she parked to turn off the phone, hoping she had given Charity enough of a trail to follow. Now, she hoped that Team Bravo was on their way to find her. Maybe she should have waited, but she was worried about what Joseph would do. There had to be some people here who really didn't under-stand what Joseph was planning. Many of the *True Believers* weren't the most intelligent. They lacked the critical thinking skills to avoid a man like Joseph Watters. He always seemed to walk away without a scratch, and his followers were ruined or dead.

Hopefully, Seth and his team would make it there before Joseph realized her money was out of reach.

She was in some kind of bedroom. It was small, with very little besides the bed and bedside table. There was no lamp, only an overhead light, and it was dark. She didn't want to turn on the overhead light because it would definitely alert people if they were in the hallway. Of course, she might make noise, even moving in the bed if she were on the second floor.

She debated moving around. She had to know where she was and how much time had passed since she'd fainted. And she needed to know more about her surroundings before checking the house.

As carefully as possible, she stood and hobbled over to the window. The throbbing from her midsection told her she had definitely bruised a rib. It wasn't the first time, so she knew what the pain was like. Of course, this was a little more intense, but she could take it. She had to until Team Bravo got to her.

Looking out the blinds, she realized she was on at least the house's second floor. Guards patrolled the area but didn't appear very good at their jobs. They were spending more time talking to each other than keeping an eye on things.

She heard the footsteps before a key sounded in the door. Well, she might not have made it out the door anyway. This way, she didn't have to fight the lock.

She expected Joseph. Instead, a man in his mid to late twenties stepped into the room. He was wearing a dark polo shirt tucked into khaki shorts. He was in good shape but more on the small side. Oh, this one was going to be a definite *True Believer*.

Short dark hair, a sharp, thin nose, and weirdly piercing

grey eyes. If he were in a horror movie, he would definitely be the creature created by the madman. There was something off about his gaze as if he wanted her to acknowledge him. Why? Did she know him?

"Summer."

"Wrong season, jackass."

His mouth turned down in a frown. God, they were all such morally corrupt assholes, but they frowned on a woman using what they deemed curse words.

"Your father is waiting for you downstairs, but he thought you might want to clean up first."

"It was then that she noticed the clothes he was holding. It looked like a dress from the nineteenth century.

"Nope."

"Excuse me?"

Jesus, these *True Believers* were a pain in the ass.

"I said I was not wearing your weird ass clothes. Just take me to Joseph."

The frown deepened. "You dishonor your father."

"My father is okay with my behavior."

Of course, Sam allowed her to be her own woman. That was Sam. She loved him for everything he was and was not. He supported her and loved her for who she was. He never told her that she owed him anything or that she was meant to bear a man's babies. He also didn't try to marry her off to his weird old friend.

He opened his mouth to say something, but she took a different tactic.

"Do I know you?"

The anger seemed to fade. "No. We never met in person, but we are related."

She blinked. "In what way? If you're talking about the cult—"

"Joyous Wave is not a cult!"

His shout was out of left field, which told her this one might be nuttier than the rest. This one took it personally.

"Either way, I'm not related to that particular insanity anymore."

He took a step forward, his hands clenched by his sides. "The insanity is you."

Okay, that made no sense, but these people rarely did.

"How so?" she asked, cocking her head to study him.

"You are destined to help us."

"That's what Joseph told you."

"Yes. That and you will be by his side to guide us."

Absolutely fucking not. But she was pretty sure saying that might have him losing his temper. Most times, she would push that anger so that he lashed out, but she was feeling a bit beaten up. She needed to draw this out as long as possible.

"Tell me everything," she said, her voice gentle. She knew from experience these idiots thought all women should be submissive.

He eyed her, suspicion darkening his looney gaze. "Why?"

"How can I know the brilliance unless I know what is about to happen?"

He sighed.

"Did Joseph order you to bring me to him right now?"

He shook his head. "He's busy."

Inwardly, she rolled her eyes. Being busy for Joseph meant one of three things: He was having sex, he was sleeping, or he was high.

"Okay, so," she said, sitting on the bed, "tell me everything."

Rami came back to the group, his feet barely making any noise. They were all good at these things, but Rami was a ghost. In fact, Seth knew that had been the former SEAL's nickname while he served.

"Four guards, but they're useless. They seem to spend more time talking than they do patrolling."

"That's odd, right?" Nikki asked.

"No. Actually, I studied this in college," Kap said. "They did a case study and pointed out that most cults would have regular members patrolling. If there was a lot of organization within the cult, they would have a good team leader. But when they are in disarray, like I assume the Joyous Wave is, they will take whoever they can get. Lots of times, it's just the biggest guys."

"Yeah," Rami said. "They're huge. Several of them look like Pacific Islanders."

"Polynesians?" Nikki asked.

Rami nodded.

"I can go in."

"Why you?" Seth asked.

"I can play lost little Hawaiian girl. If they're big and stupid, they'll fall for it."

He weighed the idea.

"And, if they don't, they will at least be distracted enough for you all to come in."

"Okay. Do it."

She took off some of her gear, handing it over to Kap, standing beside her. Seth glanced at Ryan and Maya, who watched from a few feet away. The German Sheppard was antsy since they weren't letting her go further. Her mission was to find Autumn, a person she knew by scent.

"What the hell?" Rami said, drawing Seth's attention back to the group.

Nikki was standing there with just her sports bra on.

"Listen, I don't have time to make you understand this, so I will say heterosexual men always lose their train of thought around boobs. Works every time." She grabbed her water bottle off the ground and poured some into her hand before flicking it on her face.

"This is unacceptable," Rami said, and Nikki laughed.

"Let it go, Rami. She's right," Seth said, his temper starting to fray. "We need a distraction. We can't use Maya because she will lose it if any of those assholes have Autumn's scent on them." He turned to Nikki. "Let us all get in position. The rest of TFH is on their way, but since we aren't sure what's going on in there, we need to get in there ASAP."

"Is that what Del said?" Nikki asked.

He didn't answer because he didn't ask his boss for permission. He was ready to burn the fucking world down to save Autumn. "Let's go."

"So, you are saying you're my half-brother?" Autumn asked. It was the same shit that Joseph peddled out to everyone. They all believed they had a connection to him, and that's why they were always ready to die for him.

Peter's features lit up. "Yes. Although, I do understand that you are above me."

Good God, these *True Believers* were definitely lost souls.

She understood that most people who ended up at Joyous Wave were, including her mother. But this...Joseph was a sick son of a bitch. He found these people and told them he had fathered them. Autumn was pretty sure Joseph had been shooting blanks for years. She was involved with a few survivor groups, none of whom had familial connections. All had different fathers. Autumn had paid for the DNA tests to give them peace of mind.

"I wouldn't say I was above you."

"You are so much older."

What an asshole.

"Peter? Do you think I could take a shower?"

He sighed. "I don't have permission for that."

Dammit. Peter might be a nut job, but he knew how to follow orders. Peter's phone buzzed, then he read the message. Fear filled his expression.

"Father wants to see you, and you are still wearing those clothes."

"Tell you what? Get me a washcloth to clean up my face, and I will blame the clothes on myself. Don't worry." She patted his hand.

"Are you sure?"

"I know how to handle Joseph. He'll understand."

Peter nodded, then hurried out. He forgot to lock the door, but she figured it didn't matter. Mainly because he made it back in less than two minutes with a wet washcloth. She cleaned off her face, which was difficult without a mirror, but Peter told her it was fine.

His phone buzzed again. "We must go. Father is angry."

She wanted to roll her eyes, but she smiled. "Lead the way, brother."

Autumn almost felt guilty when Peter smiled at her, but he might have had something to do with killing Freddy. She followed Peter down a hallway. The thick carpet runner muffled their footsteps as they descended the stairs into a massive living space. There, looking out the window, was the man she had sworn to kill.

"Hello, Joseph."

fifteen

SETH WATCHED as Nikki bounced up to the two massive guys chatting. Ryan was holding back because his usually well-trained dog was beside herself. She wanted to get to Autumn. Rami and Kap were taking down the other two guards.

"Oh. My. Gawd!"

Despite the situation, he couldn't fight the smile that curved his lips. Nikki was definitely good at playing an airhead.

"Where did you come from?" the one with a scar down his face asked, even while checking out her chest.

She pointed behind her. "I was out for a hike and then got sidetracked hiding from one of those big pigs."

"Boars," he said.

"I beg your pardon. Did you just call me boring?"

Nikki went hunting for boar with her brothers and father all the time.

"No. Boars. We call them boars."

"Oh," she sighed. "Thank God. I would hate to be boring."

Then she smiled at them. It wasn't her usual smile. This was calculated, but Seth knew the two men wouldn't pick up on it. They were paying too much attention to her chest.

"What the fuck does she think she's doing?" Rami muttered.

"Her job, asshole." That was Kap. Of course, Nikki was hearing all of this, but it never showed on her face.

"You're trespassing."

Her eyes widened, and she held her hand to her chest.

"I'm so very sorry. Could you help me find my way back to the trail? I would be so grateful."

He watched as both guards fell under her spell. This seemed too easy, but he would not complain.

All he cared about was getting to Autumn in time.

Autumn watched as the man she held responsible for all her worries turned to face her. Jesus, the intervening years had not been good to Joseph Watters. His once full head of hair was thinning and grey and greasy af. His once attractive face was now lined and not in that pleasing way older men looked. There were no laugh lines that told you of a good life, not like Sam. Her biological father had laugh lines that crinkled at the corners of his eyes. Years of anger and drug abuse had taken their toll on Joseph. Evil aged a person.

He was still slim but had gained a lot of weight around the middle. Those beady little eyes...those were the same. They studied her dispassionately. Oh, he was trying to look like a doting father, but she knew better. She saw the intent in his gaze.

"Summer."

"As I told your errand boy, wrong season."

He drew in a deep breath, the one that told her he was about to spout off about how she was hurting him. She definitely wasn't in the mood. Her ribs were killing her. She also just realized that her lip was split.

"If you don't mind, I need to have a seat."

Without waiting for him to give her permission, she settled on the couch. It was made of the softest of leather. There was no way this came off a factory floor. This was custom-made.

"So, let me guess...this is some *True Believer's* house."

A stony stare was his only response. That hit a nerve. Inwardly, Autumn did a little dance. It was petty to gain so much enjoyment out of poking at his ego, but she didn't care.

"I'm going to say yes." She looked over at Peter. "Someone in your family?"

"My uncle."

When she turned back to look at Joseph, he stared at her angrily. Weirdo. It was like he was trying to make her body explode into a million pieces by just staring at her. If he genuinely believed she was his child, it made him a monster. Who would look at their child like that? If she had a child, she would have nothing but love for him or her.

Wait. When did she start thinking of children? And why did she keep thinking about a little boy with Seth's eyes? Oh, damn, this was not the time to start contemplating children, especially with a man she had lied to. It was a lie of omission, but it was still a lie. And she would make a horrible mother.

Joseph must have misread her expression because he smiled. He thought Autumn was scared of him. She would have laughed in his face if the situation wasn't so serious.

"I see that you're afraid. You should be considering what you did to me. What you did to all of my followers."

She pushed the panic about children and Seth aside. If she survived this, she would definitely have to deal with it. But right now, her focus should be on the insane former cult leader.

"I was just about to turn sixteen. I didn't get them killed. You did."

She kept her voice as calm as possible. Getting upset and yelling at Joseph would escalate things too fast. She also knew remaining sedate and hiding her feelings would set off Joseph. He loved to mentally torture people.

"Your escape is what caused all my problems."

She snorted and looked at Peter. "He's wrong."

Peter was looking at her like she had lost her mind. That's fine. Maybe she had. Instead of calling her team members, she left clues in case she didn't return. Granted, she hoped they were on their way, but if not, they would be able to track her last movements. It was reckless and stupid.

She turned back to Joseph once more.

"They had no right to invade our peaceful community," he said.

"Peaceful? You were marrying preteen girls off to lecherous old men for money. You were a pimp."

She didn't understand all of it then, but thanks to her years in law enforcement, she knew exactly what was going on now. When she recounted everything to Seth this morning, it had been the tip of the disgusting iceberg of Joseph Watters, aka Donald Reynolds, and about a half dozen other names.

Joseph's beady little eyes narrowed. But he said nothing. Instead, poor, pitiful Peter decided to defend him.

"How dare you?"

Without looking over at him, she shook her head. "Don't play in the big sandbox. You would be out of your depth." She turned back to Joseph. "Do you want to tell him, or should I?"

More stoney stares. Jeez, this man hadn't changed. She had, though. She'd grown stronger, and thanks to Sam and Ian, she had learned what strong men were like. They didn't threaten or try to intimidate. They supported those around them, even women. So, the most significant change in her was that she was no longer afraid of this loser.

Her ribs were starting to throb in this position, and she was finding it more challenging to draw in a deep breath. She got up to walk around, hoping to quell some pain.

She sauntered over to the massive painting on the wall. She knew little about art but recognized a Roy Tabora original when she saw it. Definitely not Joseph's house. He would never be able to afford a print reproduction from Tabora, let alone an original like this. He would see no use in it either. He liked nice things, but only things that made him feel better, and the wonder of waves crashing against the rocks with moonlight shining down would do nothing for him.

"See, as a DEA agent, I could dig up everything they had on dear, old...Joseph here. He'd been under investigation for years, and the Feds were close to arresting him." She glanced back at the two men. "But you knew that, right, Joseph?"

"You should call him father."

A flash of movement caught her eye. The front door was to her right, with long windows bookending the large Koa wood door. She took her time turning to face the men once more. Another flash, and then she saw Nikki give her a thumbs up. She knew he had close circuit security, or maybe he didn't. If he did, no one was apparently paying attention to it. Typical

Joseph. He never paid people, so he would have volunteers handle all aspects of his security.

"Well?" Peter asked, drawing her attention away from the door. "And just so you know, Father has security everywhere. You would never make it out that door."

She cocked her head as she studied the younger man. How Peter actually thought Joseph was his father was a mystery. Granted, she didn't always think kids looked just like their parents, but they had nothing in common. Peter was at least six inches shorter than Joseph, who had always been unusually tall. He might have lost an inch, but he was still over six-four. His Scandinavian ancestors were stamped all over his stupid face.

Peter was about her height, with features that suggested Mediterranean heritage.

"I would never call him father."

Silence filled the room. She settled her gaze on Joseph. "You actually let these idiots think you fathered them all? Even Frick and Frack, who brought me in?"

"They are all my children regardless of blood."

She pursed her lips. "But Peter, he's yours."

He glanced at the younger man and smiled. Ick, it was his smarmy smile. She always thought Joseph presumed that was his loving smile. Of course, he did. He was a sociopath. It was probably pretty close to the way any serial killer looked at their prey.

"Yes. Peter is mine."

Was he lying? Did he really think he fathered children? From what they could determine, he had been shooting blanks for years. Maybe he had no idea.

"Well, there's at least one child for you to claim, although I doubt he's yours."

Joseph's head whipped around, his evil gaze narrowing on her. "You lie."

"Why would you lie like that?" Peter demanded, taking a step toward her.

She shrugged. The movement caused her a little more pain. "I'm just saying that since he's not my biological father, he might not be yours."

Seth paused in position in the hallway just out of sight. Jesus, she wasn't pulling any punches, but he couldn't blame her. She had been hunting for this asshole for over a decade.

"Fuck," Ryan muttered over the comms. He was still outside, waiting for the signal to come in. Usually, he would take Maya back to the vehicle, but they were several miles away and they might need them in case Joseph decided to run. "Joseph isn't going to like that."

He was right, but Seth understood what Autumn was doing. Stringing him along like this would give them time. He knew without a doubt that she had seen Nikki's thumbs up. He just hoped she didn't push either man too far.

"You lie," the younger man with them said.

"Nope. See, when I got out of the cult—that's what Joyous Wave was, by the way—I was rescued by an old friend of my mother's. And he helped me find out who my real biological father is. But I digress. Let's talk about how you got my mother killed, shall we? You had been under investigation for years. Illegal guns, drugs, all of it. You had your minions even trafficking girls. I might have been the catalyst, but it was a matter of time. So you faked your death and went on the run, leaving everyone to die."

"You *are* my daughter!"

Anger threaded the man's voice. Seth needed to get a look at the situation, so he peeked around the corner.

"You have to be." The young man turned to face Autumn. "He's on your birth certificate."

"Is he?" she asked, not taking her attention from Joseph.

Seth watched the young man's gaze ping-ponged between them before settling on Autumn. Seth was in an excellent position to see the man's expression. He did not like the anger. That worried him, but the jealousy he witnessed flash on the younger man's face told Seth that he was just as lethal as Joseph.

"He showed me."

She threw back her head and laughed, but there was no humor in it. It was brittle, almost broken, and his heart hurt for her. He knew this was difficult, more than anyone else would know.

"Peter, I'm sorry to tell you this, but Joseph lies. All. The. Time. He isn't my father. I didn't have an official birth certificate until I escaped. Anything he showed you is a fake." She turned to face Joseph. "Do all these idiots think you fathered them?"

Seth had an idea of where she was going with this, which wasn't a good idea. Strike that. It could drive a wedge between Joseph and Peter, but he didn't like that it made her a bigger target for both men. He knew jealousy could make a person strike out at the person they envied.

"I have many children."

Not an answer.

"We're about two clicks out," Del's voice came across the comms. "Warning, her brother is with us."

If they could, it would be best to get this done before they arrived. It was hard enough for him because he just realized the woman held his heart in her hands. If something happened to her, he wasn't sure what it would do to him.

Seth pushed those thoughts aside because he wouldn't be any better than her brother in this situation if he didn't.

"Come on. Do you really think you could father *that* many children?" He didn't respond. Instead, he walked away from her...from Peter. She sighed. "What do you want with me? I did ruin your crime operation, so is this about retribution? Gonna kill me?"

His breath backed up in his lungs. He knew Autumn was taunting him, but it didn't make it any easier to hear the woman he loved say that.

"Father would never kill you. He loves you."

She snorted. "He loves that I have millions and thinks he gets it if I'm dead."

"No! He said you would sign it over to him." The desperation in the younger man's voice was almost painful but also worrisome. Breaking his beliefs could have him lashing out.

"Then he lied. Didn't you, Joseph?"

"Father doesn't lie."

She turned toward Peter. "He does, but since you are a *True Believer*, you will never believe me, will you? No worries because I can't sign the money over to him."

"You will," Joseph said, turning to face her. It was then that he saw the gun in the man's hand.

Fuck, he had been paying too much attention to the interaction between Peter and Autumn. Not wanting to say anything, he pulled out his phone and texted Ryan.

"Joseph has a handgun, everyone," Ryan said over the comms.

"Father, this isn't what you said would happen."

Peter was going to need some therapy after this, for sure.

Another laugh. "Oh, this is precious." She sighed and turned fully to face Joseph. "See, I can't give you the money because I don't control it."

"You do. You took complete control of your money last year."

"Yep, and I put it in a trust myself. See, I knew you weren't dead. You're just a two-bit hustler, and I knew at some point you would just come find me to get the money. So, to get money out of my trust, I have to have another person sign on to release it. Without that, I can't get the money."

"You're lying."

"Fine, let me sign the papers. Then you can kill me and see that you don't get my money."

"I can petition it in court."

The glee he saw on her face worried him. He tried to get her attention, but her focus was entirely on the former cult leader.

"Go ahead. Then you'll find the DNA results that name my father. I filed those with my lawyer. And just so you know, I have good lawyers. Rich people do."

"We're closing in," Del's voice came across the comms again.

Stunned silence filled the room once more. Autumn had definitely thrown both men for a loop.

Joseph raised his arm, aiming at Autumn. "You were always a pain in the ass, Summer Joy."

"As I said, wrong season, asshole."

He couldn't see the intent in Joseph's face, but he had heard it in the other man's voice.

"Move in," he ordered as he rushed Autumn. Getting her down and on the ground would be faster than struggling with Joseph for the gun. He was sure someone else on his team would handle that.

He jumped toward her just as Joseph took his shot. He felt the burn of a bullet in his shoulder before they fell to the ground. She let out a grunt as she took the brunt of the fall.

There was a struggle behind them, and he knew his team was taking Joseph to the ground. Team Alpha came rushing into the house the next minute, along with Ryan and Maya.

"You're under arrest, asshole," Kap said.

Autumn blinked and looked up at him. He was still lying on top of her.

"I think you bruised my back."

He smiled, then he started laughing. Relief filled him, leaving him a little lightheaded. Of course, he saved her, and she complained about how he did it. But it told him she was okay if she was complaining.

He leaned down, not caring about who was there, and kissed her. He had to let her know, without words for now, how much he loved her. She said something against his lips and held herself stiff for just a moment or two before she melted. When he pulled back, she stared at him.

"I guess we have to talk about my money."

"I knew. First, we need to get things cleared up."

"Get off my sister," Ian said. Autumn smiled but said nothing. Seth rolled to his feet and then helped her up. His shoulder was throbbing, but he was sure the bullet had just grazed him. It was then that both of them heard the sounds next to them.

Rami was over by Peter, going through a bag and looking for things.

"Hold on, Peter. We're going to get you out of here. We had medical transport on standby."

Autumn hurried over and kneeled on the opposite side from Rami. Peter's shirt was dark, but it was easy to see the blood that soaked through it. Fuck, the bullet must have grazed him but then hit Peter.

"Autumn," Peter gurgled. She took his hand and held it tight.

"Hold on. Rami will make sure you get through this."

Seth wasn't sure that was the case because of the amount of blood the man was losing, but he let it go for now. There was no reason to say different.

"Make way," a booming voice said. He turned and saw the EMTs make their way through the room.

She stepped back, closer to Seth, and he fought the urge to pull her into his arms. She would never admit it, but he knew this had been hard on her emotionally.

Joseph was openly weeping like a little boy, but Autumn ignored him. Instead, she was taking complaints from her brother as they wheeled Peter out of the room.

"What do you think you were doing?" He growled the question.

"My job."

"That," Ian said, pointing toward where Joseph stood, his hands zip-tied behind him, still crying, "is *not* your job."

"Do you need my help?" he asked.

She looked at him, surprised, but then a slow smile curved

her lips. She was kind of a mess. She had a split lip—which had probably hurt when he kissed her, and she had a bruise on her jaw. But she was the most beautiful woman in the world to him.

"I got this, but thank you." Then her gaze zeroed in on his shoulder. "What the fuck, SEAL? You're shot?"

He opened his mouth to tell her he was fine, but Rami was on him.

"Take your gear off, Seth."

He wanted to argue, but Del gave Seth a look that told him the commander would order him to do it if he didn't.

Rami said something in Spanish under his breath before he pulled out some gauze and cleanser. It stung, but he didn't say anything. He just kept looking at Autumn, whose face had gone white, and her lips were a strange hue. It was odd because while he knew she cared about him, she had to have seen it was only a graze. He opened his mouth to reassure her, but the words died as he watched her eyes roll back in her head before she crumbled to the floor.

sixteen

SETH PACED BACK and forth behind the last row of seats in the waiting room at Tripler Army Medical Center. The rush to get Autumn into the hospital and figure out what was wrong felt like it had taken hours, but it had been quick. Thanks to quick thinking on Del's part, they had medical teams standing by, ready for any kind of wound.

Peter hadn't made it. The bullet had pierced an artery, and the blood loss had been too much. He knew that Autumn would probably take it hard. Not that she felt anything for the young man, but he was sure she would see him as another victim.

"You're making me dizzy," her brother said. It was about the fourth time in the last couple of hours that Ian had complained about his pacing.

He still said nothing. Had he caused the injury when he landed on her? Yes, he saved her, but at what expense? If he had hurt her, he would never forgive himself.

Ian made a rude sound as he typed on his phone. It caused Seth to pause in his steps and look at her brother.

"What?"

"This woman."

"What woman?"

"Samantha Charles."

"Oh, the Barracuda is texting you?" Charity asked, humor threading her tone. It was well-known within TFH that Ian and Samantha Charles had tangled a few times. The former CIA agent was in hiding. Seth really didn't care why or how.

"Yes. Samantha learned from Jin that my sister was injured, and she's blaming me."

The elevator door dinged open, and a rather large man with greying hair and a determined expression came striding off the lift. He was followed by a stunning black woman with long braids and the most amazing tattoos.

"Conner," Ian said, rising from the chair. "You didn't have to come down."

Conner Dillon, owner of Dillon Security, former FBI agent, and Ian's boss.

"Of course we came," the woman said. She smiled at the group and sat beside Ian and Sam. "Any word?"

He couldn't deal with this, so he started pacing again. The need to control the situation and order someone to fix the problem was like a tremor on his tongue. His hands itched to go into the operating room and perform the operation himself. Seth didn't have the training, but leaving her in the hands of another person was out of the question.

"Seth," someone said behind him, but he knew that voice. He stopped walking and looked at his team. Nikki shrugged, and that told him who had called his mother.

He turned just as his mother rushed him. She pulled him into one of her bear hugs. His wound smarted, but he didn't say anything. In all his years as a SEAL, he'd dealt with these things independently. Of course, he had never been in love with anyone before. Seeing her collapse was one of the worst things he had ever experienced—and he had been shot and stabbed multiple times.

"So," his mother pulled back, "tell us what happened."

He opened his mouth to explain when an older female doctor entered the waiting room. She wore a pair of scrubs and still wore the little hat surgeons wore.

"I'm guessing you're all the people waiting on Autumn Bradford?"

Sam stood and walked over. "I'm her father."

"First off, she's fine. She had a collapsed lung thanks to a fractured rib. We inserted a tube to inflate her lung, and she's doing well. She's unhappy that I want her to stay here at least overnight."

Her father nodded, the relief on his face easy to see. "But you're keeping her overnight."

"Yes. She's not happy about it, as I said. Truth is, I plan on keeping her for at least forty-eight hours. She's healthy, so there should be no complications, but I felt it was easier to fight the small battle over tonight. Now, on to the other business. Is there someone here that she calls SEAL?"

Everyone turned to face him. The doctor's blue gaze followed their lead and turned to face Seth.

"Ah, yes. She wanted me to tell you that it wasn't your fault. Someone had tackled her earlier in the day. She said it had been hurting for a while. I think you might have sped up her having to come in, but then, if she had been shot, she would have probably died—according to her. Also, she said she wanted to see you first."

His stomach finally settled a little bit, but his heart still felt battered. Somehow, he forced his feet to follow the doctor. Seth knew Tripler well, as they had brought people here several times that they'd rescued. They accepted civilians and military, so it was sometimes the closer hospital.

They were heading back to the ICU. While the logical part of his brain told him that it was just a precaution and it made sense, the emotional side of his brain was freaking out.

When they made it to her room, his heart seemed to settle. She looked so small and pale, but she was breathing and fine. There was a tube under her nose for oxygen. The backs of his eyes burned slightly, and he had to blink. Relief filtered through his entire body. She was fine.

"She'll have to have that oxygen on for a little while. We want to ensure her oxygen levels stay up while her lung recovers."

Her eyes fluttered open, and he watched as her gaze came to his. Relief filled her face. She held up the hand that had an IV in it. Seth took two steps, then took her hand in his.

She smiled at him, then winced. He figured that split lip was going to hurt for a while.

"Doc?" she asked without taking her gaze from his.

"Yes, Ms. Bradford?"

"Seth was grazed by a bullet and only had a quick repair job in the field before I passed out. He needs to have a doctor look at it."

"Is that true?" The doctor stepped closer and looked at his shirt. "I didn't see the blood because of your dark shirt. Come on."

He tightened his hand on Autumn's. "No."

"Don't be a baby," Autumn said. "I had a tube inserted into my lung."

She said it with such disdain he smiled. If she was feeling feisty, that meant she was feeling a little better.

"I mean, can someone look at it in here? I don't want to leave."

The doctor looked back and forth between them. "If it needs more than a couple of stitches, you must step out."

He nodded.

"Okay. Be right back."

Once they were alone, he looked down at her. "Your brother and father want to see you."

There was a long moment of silence. All the machines beeped, and he heard murmuring from the room beside them.

"So, I guess you know."

"I figured that out before anyone told me."

She sighed. "Sorry about that."

"No, you aren't."

Her lips twitched. "First, I needed you back here because I know you wouldn't have let a doctor see you."

This woman. She always took care of other people even while she was in a life-threatening situation.

"And I didn't tell you because..."

He shook his head. "We can discuss it later because the doc will return here shortly."

She nodded. He leaned down and brushed his mouth against hers.

"I love you."

Her eyes widened, and, for the first time, there was panic darkening them. She had stared down Joseph as he held a gun to her, but she looked scared when he told her he loved her. Huh. That was interesting.

"No, you don't."

"Yep. I do. You'll get used to it."

The funny thing is that he felt relief as if some enormous burden had been lifted off him. Autumn's mouth pursed, and her eyes narrowed, but she held back whatever she was about to say because the doctor returned with a nurse.

"Now, let's see that wound."

A few hours later, Seth finally let the nurse bully him into changing into some scrubs. Autumn's father had stayed with her until she had ordered him home. There was no reason for him to be there now that she was out of the woods.

As Seth followed the nurse out, he gave her a look before he slipped out the door.

"What was that look for?" Ian asked. He was sitting at the foot of her bed.

She sighed, still hating the oxygen tube. It was weird having air forced up into her nose. "He's still mad that I made him come back here and be seen by the doctor."

Ian made a rude noise. "That means I'm gonna have to be nice to him now, doesn't it?"

"What do you mean?"

"You were more worried about him, Autumn. You care about him. You didn't ask about me or Dad. You asked about him."

"He got shot."

"And you knew that Rami had taken care of it. Admit it. You care about him."

She didn't want to face that. Caring about someone was always a dangerous game, especially for the person she cared about. Joseph was gone, but the *True Believers* would probably not give up for a while. Yes, they were scattered now, but they could come back. They would blame her once again.

"Autumn."

"I had sex with him."

He made a face. "Ugh, I know."

"That's all it is. He's confused."

"Why do you say that?"

She swallowed another sigh. It was more than a little irritating that she wanted his declaration to be true. She wanted him to love her. It had never happened in her life before. Romance had been fleeting. She'd always expected that Joseph would kill her. Why get involved with someone and make them a target? It would make her a complete asshole to do that.

"He thought I was near death."

"A collapsed lung can kill you."

She rolled her eyes. "You're always so overdramatic."

"And you are trying to change the subject."

She looked away from him. "I'm not good at relationships."

He snorted. "That's a lie."

Anger surged, and she frowned when looking back at him. "What the hell?"

"You are excellent at non-romantic relationships. Also, you aren't giving Harrison credit for his feelings. I don't like the man—"

"Because we had hot monkey sex."

He frowned down at her and crossed his arms. "That man

was falling apart on the scene. The well-trained SEAL, always in control, lost it when he thought you were dying."

"That's what I mean. He's confused."

Her brother leaned down. "Stop lying. You know he cares about you."

"I'm toxic."

"Please. Who isn't in our business? One thing is that he understands that. Also, you no longer have Joseph hanging over your head. Don't belittle his feelings because you're a coward."

"Don't say that." She blinked rapidly against the burning in her eyes. She was close to crying in front of someone for the first time in years and did not like it.

"What would you call it?"

Her vision wavered, but she never got to answer him. Instead, a furious Seth stepped into the room.

"What the fuck are you doing?"

Ian gave her a smug smile before straightening and facing Seth. "Having a chat with my sister."

"You can leave now," he said, slipping between her brother and the bed, practically shoving Ian. He was protecting her again, and it was an odd feeling.

"Okay. Later."

"Ian." He turned to face her. "Samantha said hi." She knew it needled him that he couldn't find the former CIA operative.

He flipped her off but still smiled as he left them alone.

Seth was tucking the sheets around her, being a mother hen, which was...nice. Her brother had been right. She was being a coward when it came to Seth. That's why she had avoided him for months. It had been more than just her attraction to him. Deep down, he was good and would always do what was right. And he would love her so hard that it scared her.

"Sit down, Seth."

He frowned. "You aren't going to change my mind."

She knew what he was talking about.

I love you, Autumn.

"Jesus, you're difficult. Sit down, SEAL." He looked like he would refuse until she patted the mattress beside her. He did her bidding, but still looked like he wanted to argue with her.

"We haven't had time to talk, and I wanted to explain things to you."

"I don't care about your money."

She rolled her eyes. "Good God, you really are a pill. I know you don't. You have to understand that we have to go slowly."

His expression relaxed. "I can go slow."

"Really? Because we just had sex last night, and you're professing your love to me."

He shook his head. "Do you really think that's what made me fall in love with you?"

"Was it my pleasant personality or my uncomplicated family life?"

His mouth twitched, and he took her hand. "You know when I started falling for you?"

"No."

"The first time you called me SEAL."

She snorted. "If that's all it takes, you must fall in love daily."

"Stop it and listen to me, Bradford. You said it with such snark that I couldn't help but be intrigued. It wasn't that you didn't respect my service. I know how you feel about people who serve. It told me that you were no pushover. That a SEAL had to prove himself worthy of your attention, and, dammit, woman, that intrigued me."

"And so you knew you were in love with me?"

"No, Jesus, I avoided it. We work together, you are...a lot."

"Hey," she said, laughing, but she knew it was true.

"But you know what I discovered?"

"What?"

"You were worth all the trouble you brought my way. You make me laugh, and when I get too serious, you call me on it. I know you aren't ready to tell me you love me, but you will."

"Oh. My. God. You are so full of yourself, SEAL. What makes you think I love you?"

"Instead of calling your brother or father back here, you made sure I came here to see you first."

"You got shot."

"Hmm," he said. "I can wait. I'm patient."

Insufferable. "You might be waiting a really long time."

He shrugged. "Get some sleep. The better rested you are, the quicker you can get out of here."

"So bossy."

"You better believe it."

She was still smiling when she drifted off to sleep.

seventeen

THE DOCTORS at Tripler had kept her for three days. THREE DAYS. Autumn had been ready to bust herself out of there when they had finally agreed to let her go. The only way she could go was to stay with someone. Seth insisted it would be him.

"What do you mean? I can stay with my father."

Her father was already nodding, but Seth crossed his big arms over his stupid chest. He was frowning at her. She would throw something at him if he wasn't so pretty.

"I live closer to Tripler. Even at rush hour, it would take less than fifteen minutes to get back here if something should go wrong."

"Oh," her father said, looking back and forth between them before his gaze settled on her. "Love, that might be better."

She crossed her hands beneath her breasts and frowned at both men.

"I can go home and take care of myself."

"No. You can't. You had a punctured lung. You are coming home with me." He turned to face her father. "Can you help her get ready and get her downstairs? She'll have to ride in a wheelchair."

"I'm right here."

He smiled at her. "I know, but you're being irrational." He kissed her, then was gone before she could respond.

Her father chuckled.

"Shut up."

"That young man knows just how to handle you."

"He does not."

See, she could be mature.

That made her father chuckle again. "Go get changed. I don't want him reading me the riot act if we take too long."

"It'll take him forever. He probably had to park miles away."

"Do you need help?"

She shook her head as she slipped out of bed. Her father did carry the bag of clothes her brother had brought her into the bathroom. Once in there, she stared at herself for a long time. She still had a split lip, but it was on the mend. She hadn't really had a lot of rest. Did anyone rest in the hospital? They constantly checked her over, ensuring her lung was working properly. She had been off oxygen for the last twenty-four hours, which was a good sign. It was also the only reason they were letting her go home.

She couldn't wait for a shower, especially in Seth's shower. Knowing him, though, he would withhold sex. Ugh, being infatuated with a man who always did the right thing was horrible.

Infatuated was the word she was using at the moment because she didn't want to deal with any other feelings.

It took her longer than she had thought it would to get

dressed. The fact that she had spent a couple days in bed really didn't mean anything. Apparently, puncturing your lung wasn't that easy to recover from.

She heard the murmur of voices in her room. When she stepped out, her father was waiting alone, but he had a wheelchair. She frowned at it but knew they wouldn't let her go if she refused to be wheeled out in it. Also—and she didn't want to admit it to anyone—she wasn't sure she could make it outside under her own power. She was stronger, but she knew it was limited.

Her father waited in that patient way he had. With a sigh and an eye roll, she settled in the chair. He grabbed her bag, setting it on her lap. People waved as she made her way out of the hospital. They all had wanted to meet the woman who had always believed that the cult leader was alive and spent her life tracking him down for justice.

Her main problem was that so many news programs had wanted to get hold of her. They wanted her story, and she didn't want to deal with it. Thankfully, she had Jin. Through Autumn's lawyers, she let the news programs know that Jin had the exclusive story.

"You need to ease up on your young man."

"He's not *that* young."

"Age is relative to the speaker, love. You're still that skinny sixteen-year-old I met on Maui."

She sighed as the lift dinged that it had arrived. After waiting for people to depart, he wheeled her on. Thankfully, they were alone.

"He's feeling responsible."

"He is."

"See, you get it."

"What I understand is that you're running scared. You told Seth to be patient. If you're going to break his heart, let him go. No one deserves that."

She knew that he had loved his wife. From what Ian had said, they had a wonderful relationship. Autumn had been happy to know that her mother hadn't completely broken him. But every now and then, she knew he thought about the years they had lost, of never getting to see her first steps, hear her first words. That wound would never really heal.

"I don't want to hurt him."

"I know. You never want to hurt anyone. Even that Peter fellow."

She had known there had been little chance of him surviving a center-mass bullet to the chest, but it still hurt to know that he'd spent his last years on this earth with Joseph. From what they figured out, Peter had killed Freddy. Still, it was sad.

"What if I'm no good at it?"

She didn't have to explain to her father what she meant. Sam had spent the last couple of days talking to her, convincing her not to butt Seth out of her life.

"You know, your mother didn't think she deserved happiness?"

"Yeah, I know."

"That father of hers was a monster. It's why she latched onto Joseph. She wanted to fix him. The only good thing your grandfather did was leave you the trust."

It wasn't the first time she had heard that from Sam.

"What if Seth asked you to give it up?"

"Give what up?"

"All the money," he said just as the doors opened.

"He would never ask that."

"But what if he did? What if that was the one thing you had to give up to have that young man for the rest of your life?"

Sam wheeled her out the automatic doors into the weak sunlight. It was overcast today, and it looked like there had been a rain shower. She could smell plumeria dance over the wind.

"Autumn?"

Seth pulled up to the pickup spot, threw his SUV into park, and then jumped out. His gaze moved over her as if checking to see if she was all right.

"I would do it in a minute."

Sam chuckled. "That's what I thought, love."

Seth took her bag and then helped her into the car.

"Thank you," her father said, but she heard more. He had thanked all of TFH for saving her, but he had especially thanked Seth.

"Of course. You have my number, right?"

He nodded as he stepped up to the SUV. He gave Autumn a kiss on the forehead. "Rest when you get home."

Before she could tell him that she was going to Seth's house and not her own, her father shut the door and waved them off.

"You can be mad at me, but I promised everyone at work you would rest."

She still didn't like him being heavy-handed, but she decided not to say anything. She knew he was right, but she had always had a hangup admitting that she was wrong.

So, she settled back for the short ride back to his rental.

Seth glanced over at his passenger as he pulled into his neighborhood. Autumn fell asleep before they cleared the gate at Tripler. Even with the stop-and-go of traffic, she never jolted awake. That told him she was more tired than she wanted to admit.

He knew she was grumpy about coming home with him, but he could be just as stubborn as she was. When he told her he would be patient, he had been telling the truth. Still, he wouldn't let her put herself at risk. Bullying her was the only way to save face. Her father could take care of her, but he would let her do what she wanted, which meant she would try to work.

Granted, Del had told her she had to take off until the end of the month. She complained about that, too, and he knew she planned on connecting with some contacts about that Rapture drug. Joseph was in jail and was probably going to prison, but Seth had heard someone had the formula on how to make the deadly narcotic. Knowing Autumn, she would want to get it off the streets.

He pulled into his driveway. Still, Autumn slept. After putting the SUV into park and turning off the vehicle, he watched her. The fact that she was still sleeping told him everything he needed to know. Yes, she was tired, but she also trusted him.

After unlocking the front door, he returned to the SUV to get her. When he opened the door, she finally stirred.

"Come on. We're home."

The moment he said that he realized how true it was. Seth knew she wasn't ready for that. Hell, he wasn't prepared to admit it out loud, but he knew they would both have to come to terms with it in the future. Right now, though, he just needed to take care of her.

She blinked against the sunlight. Since she seemed slow to move, Seth reached across and undid her seatbelt.

"Hey. I can do that."

"I know you can."

Before she could say anything else, he slipped one arm behind her, the other under her legs, and lifted her out of the SUV.

"I can walk."

"I know you can."

"Seth."

He said nothing as he kicked the door shut and carried her into his house bridal style.

"Seth."

He looked at her. She raised her hand to cup his face. "I'm okay."

"I know. Can you shut the door?"

She did as he asked, then settled her head on his shoulder. "You know, I could get used to this, SEAL."

"That's the plan."

He started off to the bedroom, but she stopped him. "Can we just veg out on the couch and watch stupid TV? I just can't bear to sit in a bed again."

He had a massive sectional with comfy cushions.

"Okay," he said and strode over to it. After settling Autumn down, he leaned closer to brush his lips over her forehead. When he pulled back, he asked, "How about some popcorn?"

She had complained about people making popcorn and how good it smelled while she was in the hospital. When he had offered to make her some, she had refused, saying microwave popcorn sucked all the balls.

"Not microwave?"

He shook his head.

"Then yes. With butter, which I know you have because I bought it."

Had it been less than a week since they'd first made love?

"You got it."

She smiled at him and snuggled down on the sofa, and it hit him square in the chest. Again. Just seeing her here, doing things for her, was his next adventure in life.

"Well?" she asked, not taking her eyes off the TV as she flipped through the channels.

"Well, what?"

"Ya gonna make me popcorn or what?"

He smiled as he headed over to the kitchen to do her bidding. He knew if she was giving him crap, she was okay.

Several hours later, Autumn had to admit that this might have been the best plan ever. It had been a long time since she'd just watched reality TV in front of the TV. She had no idea how many housewives shows there were, but she'd been missing out.

"You really didn't know about these shows?" Seth asked.

She looked over at her companion. God, he was beautiful and good and came from a normal family. There was no way he was going to stick around with her.

"I don't have a TV. Or social media accounts."

"You don't have a TV?"

She shook her head. "Well. That's not completely true. I have one in the house in Kailua."

"In your father's house?"

Oh, damn. She forgot to mention that. "Well, I own it."

He glanced over at her. "That makes sense. Is he going to keep living there?"

She shrugged. "Not sure. Sam keeps saying he needs a flat with a view of the water. I mean, that house has a view of the water."

He nodded as if in understanding. Before Autumn could say anything else, his doorbell alarm signaled someone was at the door.

"Listen, I don't want you to get upset, but they wanted to bring you stuff. I couldn't say no."

She frowned. "What the hell are you talking about? And why would I be mad about food."

"You've been grumpy."

"I have not!"

"You have," he said almost absentmindedly.

"Seth, that's not grumpy. That's just me."

He looked up from his phone, and his gaze focused on her. Her heart tumbled a little at that attention. When he looked at her like that, she found it hard to breathe.

"But see, that's why I love you. You're okay with who you are."

She blinked rapidly just as someone rang the doorbell. "But I'm not. I'm fucked up, and my experiences in life make me a bad bet."

He leaned closer as if to make sure she couldn't look away from him. Before she could stop them, tears trickled down her cheeks. How did he do this to her with only a couple words.

"Don't worry. I like the odds."

Then he kissed her before heading to the door to let everyone in. First came Adam, Jin, and his mother, Merri. It wasn't long before the house was filled with people from TFH, her brother, and her father.

There was so much food—including her favorite fried rice from Merri. It was hours before everyone left, and Seth lifted her into his arms.

"I can walk," she protested. "I walked around all night."

"And you're exhausted." He settled her on the bed. "I'm going to make sure that everything is locked up."

He kissed her nose and then left her alone. As she waited, she thought back to her conversation with Ian.

"So, I guess this is real?" he asked.

She shrugged and looked out the sliding glass door to find Seth. He was talking with his team, laughing at something one of them said. "Not sure."

He sighed. "I told you in the hospital that he wanted forever. I think he would be good for you."

She tore her attention away from Seth to focus on her brother. "You do?"

He nodded. "Just don't throw it away because of your childhood. That would be letting Joseph win."

Her brother was right, the bastard. Ian understood her the best. He knew Joseph's mind fucking was going to bother her for years to come.

There were other things to worry about. Babies. Lots of people wanted them. She wasn't sure she did.

"Oh, no, I left you for a few minutes and you're freaking out."

She looked up just as he sat on the mattress next to her.

Maybe she had been wrong. Maybe Seth knew her better than her brother.

"It's just that you keep talking about forever and I'm not sure I'll be good at it."

"We could both be bad at it."

She shook her head. "You won't, look at you with your normal life and normal parents."

"Normal life? I grew up with two people who had to keep secrets because they were national secrets. And while my mother might have illegally peeked into my file, I couldn't tell them anything about what I was doing, and neither could my brothers. So, we weren't normal, but you know what? I understand you might be scared that I'll be better at it."

She gasped, and then he smiled.

"See. I know you. And I will wait. We don't have to discuss anything beyond tomorrow."

"But—"

"Autumn Bradford, I'm in this for the long haul. You'll get used to it."

He tugged off his shirt and cargo pants before tossing them in the laundry basket. Unfortunately, he kept his knit boxers on before climbing into bed beside Autumn. He killed the light, then pulled her into his arms.

"Now, let's get some sleep."

She traced circles on his chest, but he took hold of her fingers.

"Nope. No sex as per your doctor."

"You suck."

"I love you too."

She said nothing to that because it made her want to laugh.

Seth apparently wasn't going to let it go, and he had promised just to deal with each day as it came.

A woman couldn't ask for more than that...at least, she couldn't.

"Seth?"

"Hmm?"

"You promise you won't start discussing weddings and babies tomorrow?"

"The only wedding I will discuss is Tamilya and Marcus's wedding. The only babies are the TFH second generation, as they've started to call them. As for us, I think we don't worry about that and go to that Filipino restaurant in Kapolei you want to try out."

"Julie'z?"

"Yeah. You seemed to think that would be good."

She also made him watch a bunch of Felix and Amanda videos tonight.

"Don't you have to go to work?"

"Nope. Took off for a week. Rami will head up the team, which is good because he needs the experience of stepping in. They'll call me in if they need me."

She could hear the sleepiness in his voice, so she let go of her worries for now. He promised to go slow, and he promised her food.

For now, that was enough.

A Few Months Later

AUTUMN ROLLED HER SHOULDERS, trying to settle her nerves. There was no reason to freak out because she was moving in with Seth. Or they were moving in together would be a better way to put it.

She glanced around the apartment where she'd lived for a couple of years. It was small and looked more like a terrorist cell safe house in a Jakob Wulf movie.

The walls were bare now. All of Autumn's research had been handed over to the FBI and other agencies that had asked. She thought she would have a hard time letting go. But it had been easy. Probably because Joseph was in prison. All his assets had been frozen, so he was relying on donations and a public defender. It didn't matter if Joseph could hire the world's best criminal attorney. The mountain of evidence she had handed over was enough to keep him in prison for life. Other countries also wanted their chance to prosecute him. Joseph would spend the rest of his life in court.

Still, this was where she'd lived for so long it was hard to let go of it. It was crappy, with thin walls, and loud as hell all night long. The tenants in that building worked all kinds of hours. She was going to miss this place a little bit. And then there was the fear of this big life step.

Seth and Autumn had only been dating for three months. Hell, they had never really dated. They just fell together, and she hadn't returned to her apartment for anything other than a change of clothes. What if he regretted this and they were stuck together? She was a lot to take. Panic rose up, then sunk down into her gut.

What if she couldn't make this work because she was broken?

Just as she felt a meltdown approaching, arms slid around her stomach, then pulled her back against a hard body.

"Is everything packed up?" Seth murmured in her ear. His heat warmed her back, and that spicy scent she had always associated with him surrounded her.

"Yeah."

He kissed her temple. "What are your reasons today?"

She sighed. They might have been together for only three months, but this man knew her better than most. She turned to face him, but he kept his arms wrapped tight around her.

"I'm a lot."

"I like a challenge."

"Have you ever lived with anyone?"

"Yes."

"Your family doesn't count."

His mouth twitched. "Okay, then no, but that doesn't mean anything."

She nodded. "I just need to know."

She would have to explain what she meant to other people, but with Seth, she didn't. He seemed to understand her better than even her brother and father.

Seth cupped her face. "We need to just take it one day at a time."

Autumn rolled her eyes at the trite saying.

"Don't," he said, brushing his mouth over hers. "We can do this, Autumn. You can do this. And if we irritate the hell out of each other, we'll just be like all the other couples I know."

She sighed and leaned forward to rest her head on his chest. "Don't be charming when I'm freaking out."

He chuckled, and the sound vibrated from his chest, warming her heart.

"Come on. Let's go grab something to eat. Your dad and Merri are meeting us at Side Street Inn. Ian might even be able to make it."

"You *do* know my love language."

She leaned back and caught the concern she saw on his face. It disappeared so fast she thought she might have imagined it.

"What?"

He cocked his head.

"You're worried about something."

"Nope."

"Oh, God, you are." She pulled out of his embrace and backed away. "You're having second thoughts."

He snorted. "Not likely."

"Then, what are you worried about? And do not lie to me. I know that you're worried about something."

He opened his mouth, but she stopped him.

"Don't lie."

His mouth snapped shut, and then he sighed.

"Listen, it's just a concern that I have."

"And what would that be?"

"I know that saying the words aren't important to you. I get that, but..."

It was her turn to cock her head at him. "What words?"

Another sigh. "You don't express your feelings for me at all."

"I think I did that twice last night."

He studied her for a long moment. "Sex doesn't mean love."

She blinked, working through his comments. Seth was usually all upfront with what he was talking about. Autumn knew he understood she had issues picking up on the normal cues most people would have no problem deciphering.

"Are you questioning my feelings for you?"

He looked uncomfortable. Like he wanted to be anywhere but there.

"Listen, I just don't want to be pushy."

"We're moving in together. I think you have a right to be pushy."

Seth sighed. "You don't say 'I love you.'"

She frowned. "I don't?"

"No. And this is why I didn't want to talk about it. You don't need to say the words." He sighed. "Now it feels like I'm pressuring you."

She sighed and stepped forward. Cupping Seth's jaw with one hand, she looked into his eyes.

"Seth Harrington." She smiled. "For a man who claims to know me so well, you miss all the times I've told you I love you."

"You have never said the words."

"And you're trying so hard not to pressure me." The backs

of her eyes burned. This man was definitely too good for her, but he was stuck with her. "The words mean little to me." He opened his mouth, probably to argue that he loved her. "They do when you say them, I believe you."

"Then...why is it hard for you?"

Always so patient. "We were forced to tell Joseph we loved him. It came to mean little to me because people said it so they wouldn't be abused."

"That's fucked up."

"Yep. But I have told you without words. I told you things I have ever only told three people in my life before you. My brother, father, and therapist have been privy to my private moments with my mother. The guilt I still feel for escaping without her. The anger for keeping me away from Sam for so long."

"You really don't tell other people that?"

"They judge. It's been over fifteen years, so I should be over it, right? Or that's what I'm afraid they'll say. Then, there is the cooking."

He smiled, and she knew he was having the same memories as she had. The truth was, she loved cooking with Seth. They often prepared meals together at night. It was their routine when they were done for the day, whether it was six in the evening or one in the morning. They had odd hours, thanks to their jobs.

"And we're moving in together."

"We've been living together for three months."

"True, but this is official. I don't let people in my spaces, and I definitely don't cry in front of people like I do with you. I feel safe with you." Then, knowing he needed the words, she stopped being a coward. "I love you, Seth Harrington."

His eyes darkened as he stared down at her. His love for her was easy to read. "I love you."

"How could you not? I mean... I'm drama-free and have an easy backstory."

His mouth twitched. "Yeah. I really hate that we're meeting your dad for lunch."

"Yeah, and this is no place for a quickie. We'll eat fast, then we'll do wonderful things to each other later."

He kissed her nose. "Deal."

Ian looked down at his phone and frowned. He wasn't in the mood to deal with his sister or her newest way to torment him: bringing up Samantha Charles—or whatever her real name was.

The call was from an unlisted number.

Well, that meant it was Samantha Charles. And why was she calling him? She usually sent him mocking texts.

Just let it go to voicemail.

That was the smarter thing to do. She tormented Ian on so many levels that hearing her voice brought about conflicting emotions. He wanted to hunt her down and turn her over to authorities. He knew her ex-employer—the CIA—wanted her brought in. But a part of him also knew something else was going on. Something that reeked of a cover-up.

When his phone stopped vibrating, he slipped out of his car. He'd parked at the lot adjacent to Side Street Inn. Seth had insisted that this was a family lunch, and unless work kept him away, Ian needed to be there. He rolled his eyes. Captain America was annoying—although Ian was happy for his sister. In all the years he'd known Autumn, Ian had never seen her quite this content. Seth seemed to have chased away the sadness.

When his phone vibrated again, he pulled it out of his pocket. Unknown, again. She didn't leave a voice message but instead called him again. He rolled his shoulders, and he clicked to answer against all of his training and better judgment.

"Finally," the deep, sultry voice said. He didn't know if Samantha was from the American South or if she was faking the accent. Either way, it was his kryptonite.

"I was busy."

"You were sitting in your car goofing off."

"I was not goofing—" then what she said struck him. "How did you see me?"

"I snuck into your car and put in cameras."

She could do it, but he knew she wouldn't. "Right."

She snorted. "I tracked you with the traffic cams, and since I know y'all are going to lunch today, I wanted to talk to you before you went in. You're not good at hiding things from your sister."

"What are you trying to hide from Autumn?"

"Not really hide. I just want an embargo because Autumn should have a good weekend without my shit. Just tell her that I'm disappearing for a while."

Alarm lit through him. Samantha might go underground, but she usually didn't break off all contact for long. She would just establish herself in a new location.

"What do you mean you're disappearing?"

"Aw, look at you faking worry. Nothing big. Just have to make sure I'm not being followed. Don't worry, MI-6, I can handle it."

It still bothered him. His time with the British spy agency

taught him that being out on your own was a bad place to be, no matter how bloody brilliant you were. Sometimes, the smartest of them made the stupidest moves.

"You need to talk to Jin Phillips."

"I did. I just couldn't wait any longer, and I wanted you to know so your sister could find out. That's all I have, Mix."

"Don't call me that."

"Oh, God, when you get that prissy tone, it just turns me on so much." Her husky chuckle wound through him. Fuck, why was he so damned hot for a woman who mocked him like she did? "Just wait until after this weekend. We both know your sister hasn't had many happy moments like this, and I don't want to be the storm cloud. I'll probably be back online in a week or two."

And that's why he couldn't completely dismiss her. She cared about people, especially those associated with Task Force Hawaii.

"Okay, fine. Just..."

His voice trailed off as he searched for something to say. There was nothing to say and no reason to be freaking out that she might disappear and never be seen again. He barely knew the woman.

"What?"

"Check back in with Autumn as soon as you can. She'll worry."

"Oh. Okay. I will. Probably will just be a week or two."

The line went dead. Why did Ian feel a sense of loss? They didn't talk, and they barely texted. He drew in a deep breath, slipped his phone back into his pocket, and continued to the restaurant.

The woman known as Samantha Charles watched Ian Smith walk into the restaurant. For a former spy, he was terrible at picking up he was being followed. She guessed it was due to the idea that he no longer had people gunning for him.

What did that feel like?

She pushed that thought aside and continued past the restaurant. None of them would recognize her unless she talked. Her usually curly hair had been tamed and put up under a jet-black wig. She had been cursed with two different colored eyes, which she hid behind brown contacts that were a pain in the ass, but much needed in this case. She'd used lighter makeup on her skin to hide her usually olive undertone. Being the granddaughter of an actress had helped her conceal her identity these past few years.

What was it like to have lunch plans? She had been like that once, but her old life dissolved because she decided to be a whistleblower. Her fiancé had dumped her, and her other hacker friends had shunned her. The only people she trusted all lived in Hawaii, and they barely knew her.

Shaking off her morose thoughts, she headed down the street. Even though it was small, Hawaii had a lot of hiding places. It was time to disappear entirely off the grid as Samantha Charles—even if just for a few weeks.

Thank you so much for reading ***Justified Secrets!*** I hope you enjoyed the first book in the series. There will be more coming in 2025 starting with Justified Fear. To be one of the first to find out all about the book, be sure to subscribe to my newsletter or website news (or both!).

If you want to get to know the original Task Force Hawaii team, make sure to check out all the books available in digital, print, and audio!

And, I'm sure you want to know what is coming up for Ian Smith and the mysterious Samantha Charles. Well, they will be the first book in brand new Harmless World Series, Dillon Security. ***Never Trust a Spy*** will release late Spring 2025.

If you loved Autumn and Seth's story, please think about leaving a rating or review at your favorite online store.

acknowledgments

Every book takes a ton of people to get it out. Big thanks to Scott Carpenter for the beautiful design for the new Task Force books. You always know exactly how to create what I want.

Thanks to Noel Varner for working hard on the edits. It was down to the wire for this one, so thanks a lot for your help.

Thanks to my readers who have asked for this book. A lot of you wanted this story so I hope you enjoy the story.

Brandy, girl, you keep me sane. Or I guess we could say, somewhat sane,

And last but not least, thanks to my family. Les and my girls (human and the furry brown one), you keep me going when I want to quit. Thanks for always believing in me.

For those of you who are wondering about Amanda and Felix videos, you can check them out on their YOUTUBE CHANNEL. They go to a lot of locally owned places on Oahu and they are so much fun to watch.

You can also check out Roy Tabora's art.

k out faith—>

Coming in November with a new epilogue.

Jensen Wulf had no idea the one woman he could never live without in business was the woman he needed in his bed. He just has to convince the contrary woman he loves her.

Four years ago

Jensen Wulf let himself into his New York brownstone and sighed with relief. It had been a long three months since he'd been here, in what he had termed as his *sanctuary*. He'd left on his own accord, ready to make a fresh start and walk away from the heroin haze he'd lived in over the last four years.

The apartment smelled fresh. The vinegary scent of heroin no longer clung to the furniture. He assumed that his mother had made sure everything had been cleaned out before he returned.

She was good like that. She kept things tidy, even as everything else was falling apart. The floors had been redone, there was a new coat of paint throughout...damn, he owed her.

He had disappointed her, more than a few times, but almost dying of an overdose was the worst. He would never forget the look of pain in her gaze. It was that look that had made him realize he wasn't just hurting himself.

There was mail stacked up on a credenza. His mother had taken care of the bills, he knew that. But, he was sure there was other correspondence for him. He picked up the envelopes and stepped into the living room.

He didn't see her at first. She was sitting in the chair to the right of the fireplace, her phone in her hand as she read something on the screen.

"I thought you would never make it in here."

American, but there was a slight accent to her voice that he couldn't place. She was dressed in a striking red blouse, a short black skirt, hose, and fuck me heels. Her hair was dark brown and long from what he could tell. She had it up in a ponytail. A black coat was draped over the arm of the chair.

"Excuse me?"

She looked up at him. Ice blue eyes. Jesus, it didn't fit with the rest of the package.

"You spent a lot of time in the foyer."

He opened his mouth to explain why, then he remembered it was *his* fucking house.

"Who the hell are you?"

She smiled, but there was little humor behind it.

"Nicola McCann."

The name was familiar, but he was sure he had never met her.

"And you are sitting in my house for what reason?"

"Your mother hired me."

"For what?"

"I'm your sober companion. We're going to be best friends for the next three months."

about the author

From an early age, USA Today Best-selling author Melissa loved to read. When she discovered the romance genre, she started to listen to the voices in her head. After years of following her AF Major husband around, she is happy to be settled in Northern Virginia surrounded by horses, wineries, and many, many Wegmans.

Keep up with Mel, her releases, and her appearances by subscribing to her NEWSLETTER. If you want to keep up with cover reveals, new behind the scene info on her writing, and when new excerpts are posted, follow her MelissaSchroeder.net News News. Or you can do both! They are low traffic, so you will not get tons of emails.

Check out all her other books, family trees and other info at her website!
If you would want contact Mel, email her at: melissa@ melissaschroeder.net

instagram.com/melschro

amazon.com/author/melissa_schroeder

facebook.com/MelissaSchroederfanpage

bookbub.com/authors/melissa-schroeder

goodreads.com/Melissa_Schroeder

tiktok.com/@melissawritesromance

Printed in Great Britain
by Amazon